MODE *series directed by Maria Luisa Frisa*

James Sherwood

The London Cut

Savile Row Bespoke Tailoring

Marsilio MODE FONDAZIONE PITTI DISCOVERY

This volume has been published in occasion of the exhibition
The London Cut: Savile Row Bespoke Tailoring,
a project by Fondazione Pitti Discovery
Palazzo Pitti, Florence, January 4 – February 10, 2007

The author would like to thank and acknowledge the following without whom the project *The London Cut* would not have been possible: Raffaello Napoleone, Lapo Cianchi, Sibilla della Gherardesca, Maria Luisa Frisa, Luca Trevisiani, Franca Tancredi, Anna Pazzagli, Francesca Tacconi, Sybille Bollmann, Amanda Montanari, Federica Cimatti, Lisa Chiari, David Harvey, Peter Ackroyd and Patricia Carruthers. In addition to all of the guv'nors, cutters and tailors of the Row named in this book, the following have been guardian angels of *The London Cut*: Don Rouse, Gavin Davis, Gill Godfrey, Lara Mingay, Poppy Charles, Anna-Marie Scott, Rowland Lowe-Mackenzie, Chris Modoo, Francesca Leon, Maddy Platt, Claudia Ottobrino, Francesca Leon, Marie Scott, Petter & Anthony @ Spencer Hart, Tiffany @ Ozwald Boateng, Shivaun @ Mark Powell. For exhibition loans: Janet Taylor, Tom Ford, Whitney Bromberg Hawkings, Lord & Lady Montagu of Beaulieu, Jackie Bethel @ Lord Montagu's office, Derek & Sacha Rose, Sebastian Horsley, Celia Birtwell, Susan Farmer, Lady Bamford, Hamish Bowles, John Hunter Lobb, Sarah Webster, Vicky Williams & all at Cleverley. Finally: Simon Hesling, Tessa Salmo, Judy Bennett, Lee Brown, Anthony Keegan, Chris Skelton, Jane Hurring, Lynda Gandy, Edith Gandy, Mr & Mrs R Sherwood and Hilda Sherwood, all of whom have aided me during my adventures on Savile Row.

graphic design and lay-out
Alessandro Gori.Laboratorium

editorial coordination
Federica Cimatti

editing
Aaron Maines

Fondazione Pitti Discovery apologizes and is available
if any photographic credits have been unintentionally omitted

© 2007 by Fondazione Pitti Discovery
www.pittimmagine.com

© 2007 by Marsilio Editori® s.p.a.
in Venice
www.marsilioeditori.it

First edition: January 2007
ISBN 88-317-9155

Distributed in the UK and Europe by
Windsor Books
The Boundary
Wheatley Road
Garsington Oxford OX44 9EJ
tel 01865361122 fax 01865361133

Distributed throughout the rest of the world by
Rizzoli International Publications
300 Park Avenue South,
New York, NY 10010
tel 2123873400 fax 212383535
www.rizzoliusa.com

Printed by Grafiche Nardin, Ca' Savio - Cavallino - Treporti (Venice) for Marsilio Editori® s.p.a. in Venice

CONTENTS

Savile Row has been the route to excellence in men's tailoring for the past two hundred years. Revolt, revolutions and reform in men's clothing have always been obligated to use the shops along this street in London's Mayfair district as a point of reference. The tailors, cloth, cut, stitching, the details of suit construction, the trends, fame, wealth and class—both social and individual—of their clients have all been envied, copied, abhorred, negated, overturned.

The project that Pitti Immagine and the Fondazione Pitti Discovery have created for the Row is much more than a simple recognition of the origins of men's fashion: it is acknowledgment that the Row's rules for men's tailoring continue to survive and thrive today. Savile Row tailors still create superb classic clothing for the *crème de la crème* (a variegated, but no less noble category in our day and age, comprising everything from soccer players to rock stars). Their clothing remains a creative inspiration and an example of craftsmen's mastery for many young fashion designers. Tailoring and handmade clothing for individual clients—in other words bespoke elegance—remain fundamentally important issues today. They are nothing less than the expression of a typically European production and design culture. The current regeneration (in its literal sense: generational change) of London tailoring is an important sign for all those who have chosen this craft, even in Italy, which can vaunt an equally glorious tradition. Not by chance, there is also a great deal of Italy on the Row: most of the cloth used for bespoke clothing comes from the best Italian producers.

This is an epochal moment for European fashion, and for Italian clothing design in particular, the strongest on the old continent. If production in emerging countries earns consistent margins, and is pushing for higher levels of quality as well, then the path to absolute excellence is the best way not only to respond to this challenge, but to raise the stakes as well. This is precisely what the best Italian companies and Savile Row Bespoke—a collective group of tailors, each with his own history and strong individual identity—are doing: defending the past while looking forward and projecting their business onto a global scale.

RAFFAELLO NAPOLEONE
CEO, Pitti Immagine

Savile Row is a unique street. Located in the heart of Mayfair, just yards from the luxury retail of Bond Street and the sweeping majesty of Nash's Regent Street, it is a hidden gem. Here over one hundred working tailors practice an art that goes back over centuries and in the adjoining square mile there are dozens more.

Savile Row's history stretches back to the eighteenth century when the street we know as the Row was a vegetable garden in the grounds of Burlington House (now the Royal Academy of Art). The present home of Gieves & Hawkes, no. 1 Savile Row, was built as a private house whose guests included the infamous George "Beau" Brummell: the definitive Regency dandy. The first tailors moved in at the very birth of the nineteenth century.

In 2003 Savile Row Bespoke was formed, an organization whose founding members are five of the great houses on the Row: Anderson & Sheppard, Dege & Skinner, Gieves & Hawkes, Henry Poole and Huntsman, all of whom have traded for over one hundred years. SRB aims to protect and to promote the art of bespoke tailoring on Savile Row. The group now embraces the new tailors on the Row, all of whom are represented in *The London Cut: Savile Row Bespoke Tailoring* at Palazzo Pitti. SRB enjoys links with the schools and colleges training tomorrow's designers and craftsmen. It will continue to ensure that Savile Row remains not just a name but a thriving community and a world respected standard: the gold standard of handcrafted tailoring.

What is Savile Row's future? It lies, of course, in the luxury tailoring market; a market where brand leviathans are falling over each other to build "brand credibility," "individuality," "authenticity" and "craft roots" . . . all of which thrive and survive quietly here at Savile Row. Today Savile Row is more than a piece of history. It is a standard, an inspiration and a community. We thank all of those who have given us the opportunity to give you an insight into what Savile Row truly means today.

MARK HENDERSON
MD of Gieves & Hawkes
Chairman of Savile Row Bespoke

INTRODUCTION

ADVENTURES ON SAVILE ROW:
AN OBSERVATION

Is there another street where the history and mystery of men's style meet as grand as London's Savile Row? I think not. The spiritual home of bespoke tailoring for two centuries, Savile Row is the only street in the world where you'll see the Duke of Devonshire walking up the east side of the street for an appointment with his tailor while notorious Babyshambles lead singer (and consort of Kate Moss) Pete Doherty staggers down the west side to be measured up for his first bespoke suit.

Traditionally, Savile Row has served the cult of celebrity quietly and with discretion. When asked if he would divulge the names of his celebrity clientele, Angus Cundey (MD of Henry Poole & Co. and "Godfather of Savile Row") will answer with a twinkle in his eye, "Let me see. Will Churchill do? Or perhaps Emperor Napoleon III? Maybe Dickens?"

Suffice it to say, everyone who is anyone in world history—politicians, film stars, heads of state or fashion icons—is dressed on Savile Row: Admiral Lord Nelson, the Duke of Wellington, Rudolph Valentino, Pablo Picasso, Marlene Dietrich, Fred Astaire, Frank

Sinatra, Sir Laurence Olivier, Alfred Hitchcock, Cary Grant, H.M. the Queen, John Lennon, Mick Jagger, Gianni Versace, Madonna, Jude Law and Daniel Craig to name a very few.

Yet Savile Row has until the past decade persisted in protecting the identity of its star customers and has famously professed a superb indifference to the fashion industry. "We tradesmen have customers," proclaims Dege & Skinner chairman Michael Skinner, "The professions—tarts and solicitors—have clients."

Bespoke tailoring is a mysterious and secretive art that stands above and beyond all other forms of men's suiting. As Savile Row will tell you, a bespoke suit is created for the individual on an exclusive basis. The customer is measured by hand, his pattern is cut by hand and the garment is then sewn by many hands with an average of three intervening fittings on the customer. The entire process takes an average of fifty-two hours manpower and three months from ordering to delivery. Any tension between the tailor's innate style and the customer's requirements must be resolved. The result? A suit that compliments the man and the house that produced it.

While Savile Row discreetly practiced its craft, debate has been raging around it in the fashion industry as to the nature of luxury in the context of global brands. Momentum has been growing to reject the fantasy that luxury labels opening internationally branded outposts worldwide with all the profligacy of McDonald's can possibly be worthy of the word. True luxury, or quality, is to be found in idiosyncratic family-owned firms that champion discreet personal service above celebrity wannabe culture and produce handmade goods tailored to a discerning individual's needs. Such is the history of bespoke tailoring and thus the time is right to applaud it: despite the fact that this attention has taken some of the older houses by surprise.

Running parallel to this revived appreciation for quality and craft is a renewed interest in great British heritage brands led by Burberry's renaissance under Rose Marie Bravo and Christopher Bailey. Pringle of Scotland, Aquascutum and Daks have all capitalized on the puree of fashion and nostalgia that has powered Burberry into pole position on the world stage. The more fashion-forward Savile Row tailors witnessed Burberry's success and saw no reason why houses higher on

the quality food chain shouldn't emulate it. The older houses saw
their values being hijacked and—not a little indignant—resolved to
reclaim the word "bespoke" for true craftsmen. As a global brand, few
names are as potent as Savile Row: the street synonymous with
bespoke tailoring and birthplace of the "London Cut." Burberry may
wrap itself in the Union Flag and try to corral "Britishness" as
a brand value, but they do not have a monopoly.

The square mile surrounding Savile Row—the synonym for the
tailor's quarter in London's aristocratic Mayfair district—has endured
both good and bad fortune over the last two hundred years. The
oldest firm on the Row, Henry Poole & Co., was founded in 1806
while Ede & Ravenscroft on neighboring Burlington Gardens is
England's oldest family owned tailor, first established in 1689.
Similarly, Savile Row legends Anderson & Sheppard, Davies & Son,
Dege & Skinner, Huntsman, Kilgour and Welsh & Jeffries can trace
their tailoring bloodline back way beyond a century each.

Between them, the Savile Row tailors have dressed practically every
man of consequence (and some of no consequence or credit) since the
turn of the nineteenth century. It is slightly ironic that the
profession's name—"tailor"—is derived from the French *tailler* (to
cut). It is equally telling that Italy has chosen to applaud Savile
Row's achievements with the January 2007 Pitti Uomo exhibition,
The London Cut, held at the Palazzo Pitti in Florence. One may
conclude that perhaps the men who love English tailoring the most
are least likely to be Englishmen. English bespoke tailoring owes
about 80% of its turnover to international trade. To be fair,
a proportion of these men are English expats.

As Ralph Lauren has proved, the Savile Row style is a valuable source
of inspiration for foreign designers as well as buyers. But however
efficiently designers such as Ralph Lauren translate the London Cut
into ready-to-wear, the respect the world feels for Savile Row bespoke
is unshaken. Countess Sibilla della Gherardesca, recalls her
granduncle the Count della Gherardesca ordering all his shirts from
Jermyn Street and sending them back to London to be laundered.
The story echoes one of the many anecdotes surrounding Regency
dandy George "Beau" Brummell, man of fashion and sartorial advisor
to the Prince Regent (later King George IV), who insisted on sending

his linens to Islington Fields to be dried so they would not gather soot spots as they would if hung near Brummell's Mayfair townhouse on Chesterfield Street.

You will hear many such echoes on the Row. Alan Bennett, owner of venerable Savile Row tailor Davies & Son, acquired a navy and black suit, shirt, tie and loafers at the 1997 Sotheby's sale of the late Duke of Windsor's estate. The Duke was a loyal customer of Davies & Son and Bennett has a file of paper patterns relating to the Duke when he was still Edward, Prince of Wales in the thirties. While Bennett was showing me these treasures, a patrician gentleman came into the shop for a fitting. I was later told that his father was King Edward VIII's equerry during the abdication crisis of 1937 when the King renounced his throne, married "double divorcee" Wallis Simpson and became the permanently exiled Duke of Windsor.

With the weight of history bearing down on any man who cares to walk down Savile Row, it is understandable that it has gained a reputation as a forbidding street for any chap who isn't a military man, a skilled equestrian or blue-blooded. Bespoke tailoring appears to be a closed world where the tailors often seem grander than their customers and the notion of fashion is looked upon with the same disdain as ill breeding. Mr. John Hitchcock, wise and witty MD of Anderson & Sheppard, recalls that the shop would close at 5 o'clock sharp regardless of the fact that it left the odd Viscount banging his umbrella on the window at five minutes past the hour.

But the Row has reacted to criticism of its aloofness and archaic demeanor as far back as 1965 when society photographer and celebrated dandy Cecil Beaton fired a warning shot across the bows of Savile Row: "It is ridiculous that they should go on turning out clothes that make men look like characters from P.G. Wodehouse. I'm terribly bored with their styling, so behind the times. They really should pay attention to the fashion produced by the young Mods . . . the barriers are down and everything goes. Savile Row has got to reorganize itself and, to coin a banal phrase, get with it." Hardy Amies, haute couturier to H.M. the Queen residing at no. 14 Savile Row, famously bought mod suiting but had the garments remade on Savile Row. Amies's point was that though nobody could surpass Savile Row for craft, fashion had long since left the street behind.

Savile Row didn't heed its critics until the advent of Tommy Nutter in 1969. The opening of Nutters of Savile Row on Valentine's Day 1969 marked the beginning of the end for frosted windows and frosty service on Savile Row. Though new generation tailor Timothy Everest (a Nutter alumnus) recalls the windows of Norman of Savile Row being shrouded in a funereal curtain as late as 1987, tailors such as Henry Poole immediately followed Tommy Nutter's lead with clear glass windows and displays calculated to welcome men into the shop rather than keep them out.

Savile Row did indeed get hip helped by the brief, gaudy hour in the late sixties and early seventies when maverick tailors Tommy Nutter, Mr. Fish and Blades brought the boutique concept to bespoke's heartland. Swingers such as The Beatles, Mick Jagger and Elton John were proud to be named as Savile Row bespoke customers. Mick and Bianca Jagger were married in matching white Tommy Nutter three-piece trouser suits, as were Lord and Lady Montagu of Beaulieu and John Lennon and Yoko Ono. This golden age was recorded by men's tailoring journals such as *Tailor & Cutter*, *Men's Wear* and *Man About Town*.

As the seventies progressed, the aforementioned magazines recorded Savile Row struggling once again to please grassroots customers and attract the younger generation. By the time Giorgio Armani launched himself onto international male fashion consciousness as modeled by Richard Gere in *American Gigolo* (1980), Savile Row did indeed flounder. Armani's soft, unstructured suits were cut in what Savile Row would consider dress rather than tailoring fabrics. "Anderson & Sheppard is known for a softly tailored cut but our suits are portraits in cloth and precisely fit the customer. What Armani did—quite brilliantly—was make suits that didn't fit fashionable," says Anderson & Sheppard MD John Hitchcock.

Richard James, one of the trio of Savile Row tailors who would be christened the "New Establishment" when they emerged in the early nineties, recalls Armani's dominance of the *Dynasty* decade. "Armani is a hero of mine. His early collections revolutionized men's tailoring. He did serious damage to Savile Row. The sons of Savile Row customers weren't interested in bespoke once Armani came along. It was a major culture shock. Whereas once fathers introduced their sons to their bespoke tailor as a rite of passage, now the sons were introducing daddy to Armani."

It took another decade for Savile Row to rally with new names above the door such as Ozwald Boateng and Richard James. This new blood was at first unwelcome but ultimately critical to the survival of bespoke tailoring on the Row. Richard James was the first of the new generation bespoke tailors to open a shop front on Savile Row in 1992 and take the radical step of opening his shop on a Saturday. Some of his august neighbors grumbled and glowered because they thought he didn't make the cut as a bespoke tailor. His orders were not made on the premises or by cutters employed exclusively in-house. Ozwald Boateng's imperial purple suits with acid yellow silk linings were greeted with derision until they quickly became a cult hit with movie stars and city boys alike.

Ozwald Boateng's standalone shop opening on Vigo Street in 1993 saw the new establishment literally top and tail Savile Row. Boateng should not be compared to Tommy Nutter, but his genius for self-publicity does echo that of the late great man. Like Nutter, Boateng recognizes the unique relationship tailor and customer forge. "In the bad old days there was a lot of tugging at forelocks and toadying to the customers. But now a man looks up to his tailor. He's a sartorial psychiatrist who knows all the secrets and socializes in the same world." There can be little doubt that had Nutter been around today he too would be the star of his own cult reality TV show as Boateng is with *House of Boateng* on Robert Redford's Sundance Channel. The notorious Mr. Nutter lured the third member of the trinity, Timothy Everest, onto the Row as a teenager in the eighties when the cute, impressionable young man answered a newspaper advertisement reading "boy wanted." But when the time came for Everest to open his bespoke tailoring business in 1991, he eschewed the Row in favor of a Georgian townhouse in London's East End with the caveat "Savile Row? It would be like moving back in with my parents." In 1997, Everest, Boateng and James were photographed for *Vanity Fair* as figureheads of "Cool Britannia"; simultaneously stealing the old guard tailors' thunder and re-energizing the Row.

What a difference a decade makes. A renewed sense of collective purpose gripped the Row for the first time in its checkered history,

coming to a head in 2006. New firms such as Richard Anderson (co-founded by Huntsman man and master tailor Brian Lishak, who has clocked fifty years on the Row) and Spencer Hart (founded by Nick Hart) thrived on the Row. *AngloMania*, the 2006 exhibition of great British style at New York's Metropolitan Museum curated by British-born Andrew Bolton, dedicated a room to Savile Row tailoring and united old and new generation houses under the bespoke banner. 2006 could well go down in Savile Row's history as the year when the home of bespoke tailoring fought back from near extinction. In an unprecedented move, the big beasts of the Row (Henry Poole, Gieves & Hawkes, Dege & Skinner, Hardy Amies, Anderson & Sheppard and Huntsman) joined forces to form Savile Row Bespoke: an organization that protects and promotes Savile Row. Though formed in 2004, SRB really got its motor running last year under the leadership of Gieves & Hawkes MD Mark Henderson.
Richard Anderson, Ozwald Boateng, Richard James, A.J. Hewitt, Hardy Amies and Norton & Sons (the company with the youngest guv'nor on the Row: 34-year-old Patrick Grant) have all rallied to the cause: saving Savile Row from the three-headed beast of crippling rent rises, aging talent and shyster tailors who trade on the name but don't meet the standards of Savile Row bespoke tailoring.
The first head has been effectively severed. As SRB chairman Mark Henderson thundered at a critical moment in rent negotiations, "Savile Row (is) the international home of bespoke tailoring: thriving, defiant and here to stay." A Westminster Council report (what Henderson calls "a lifeline for the bespoke tailoring industry") revealed that landlords Pollen Estate had already upped rents on the Row by 57% in the last decade. Thanks to Westminster Council's directive, the tailors on the golden mile will be cushioned from the threat of Bond Street-sized rent hikes or eviction. But short leases and new fashion brand faces on the Row still haunt the tailors' future.
What Henderson and his cohorts want to protect as much as their valuable Savile Row shop fronts are the onsite workrooms that are the true hallmark of bespoke tailoring. Pressure has been brought to bear on the landlords to sacrifice the higher rents they could charge by turning workrooms into offices or retail space. This is necessary in order to protect the integrity of this unique street.

Savile Row currently employs over one hundred tailors, with dozens more operating in the West End. As Henry Poole chairman Angus Cundey points out, a Savile Row tailor trains for ten years, "longer than a doctor." These men (and increasingly women) are the lifeblood of the Row. They are the ones who make a little piece of English heritage for an average £3,000 for a two-piece suit. Compare this to £20,000 for a Brioni coat with a chinchilla collar or an Alexander McQueen leather jacket for £6,000 and you begin to appreciate why Savile Row should be cherished.

Savile Row has rarely been in better shape than it is in 2006; turning over an annual £21 million collectively for roughly 10,000 bespoke suits. As Henderson points out, everyone from Tom Ford to Jude Law are customers. Recently fashion brands such as Calvin Klein, Ralph Lauren, Paul Smith, Manolo Blahnik and *Vogue USA*'s Andre Leon Talley and Hamish Bowles have all tasted the heaven that is Savile Row bespoke, just as Bill Blass, Gianni Versace and Valentino did in their day. If fashion recognizes Savile Row's supremacy then what does this tell you?

"It would be hugely detrimental to our heritage to lose one of our oldest institutions," says Henderson, "but we are not preserved in aspic. Savile Row wants to adapt to the times. But it doesn't want to be moved from its iconic address by multinational fashion brands." The brands he has in the back of his mind are Hackett, The Duffer of St. George and Jil Sander, all of which tried to open on Savile Row and ultimately made swift exits. "Can't hack it," as Michael Skinner says with a wry smile.

The latest newcomer is Abercrombie & Fitch who contentiously announced the opening of their first London flagship on Savile Row in September 2006. The tailors questioned the wisdom of opening a superstore for "American frat boy style" in a former Mayfair mansion rather than on the much more commercial Regent Street where Brooks Brothers opened in September 2006. At the time this introduction was being written, Abercrombie had yet to open its doors and the gargantuan billboards slathered with naked male torsos had been reduced by 50% after complaints from local residents and shopkeepers.

"They come and they go," Henderson says, ambiguous as to whether he means Abercrombie's abs or the shop itself. "Exploiting the Savile Row name to attract high paying retailers and businesses at the cost of this world-esteemed industry is short sighted." The prime new site on Savile Row is no. 5, and companies as diverse as Dunhill, Giorgio Armani and Tom Ford have been rumored to be taking the shop front between Kilgour and Gieves & Hawkes. Time will tell. Suffice it to say that many of the British bespoke tailors who belong on the Row will have shop fronts there come Spring 2007.

A serious danger to bespoke tailoring still exists on Savile Row with firms (largely on the west side of the street) who advertise "bespoke suits for £400." These bootleg garments, largely manufactured overseas, are cuckoos nesting on Savile Row's reputation. As Nick Hart, proprietor of Spencer Hart, told me for a *Financial Times* feature in July 2006, "Savile Row is one of the last craftsmanship businesses that represents British excellence in the modern world. It has real relevance. These companies are parasites and their suits are knocked-up in China. Savile Row can't afford to be complacent. At the moment it is all a bit too much like a Monty Python sketch— another British cottage industry standing on the deck of the Titanic drinking Pimms and denying the realities of the modern world."

To be fair to the west side (where Spencer Hart it also situated), 40 Savile Row (the name of the business as well as the address) launched a full bespoke service in October 2006 with a respectable starting price of £2,200 and the promise that "the process takes four to five weeks with a minimum of three fittings" and an assurance that "the tailor takes up to eighty hours to make the suit." Reducing the cost and the time to produce a bespoke suit is canny on 40 Savile Row's part, but neither would be possible without cutting some corners. The garment may still be factory-made abroad.

Hart offers the caveat that "playing Devil's advocate, a perfectly fitted bespoke suit in a very expensive cloth in the wrong style, color, pattern and trimmings remains a horrible garment. It just fits well." Carlo Brandelli, the creative director of Kilgour, had drawn the same conclusion before performing an extreme makeover on Kilgour's Savile Row store in 2003 and presenting bespoke tailoring in a twenty-first century high fashion context. The modernization of Kilgour, comparable to Tom Ford's turnaround of Gucci on a much more modest scale, has attracted dashing twenty-first century blades such as Bryan Ferry, Jude Law, Rankin and Michael Owen to Savile Row. The proposition that Kilgour may be hanging the success of made-to-measure and ready-to-wear collections on the house's reputation for bespoke is not a criticism. Parisian couture houses Christian Dior, Chanel and Jean Paul Gaultier are no strangers to loss-leading, elite, handmade collections that bestow prestige on a brand and ultimately sell satellite products. Savile Row Bespoke will often evoke haute couture or champagne as comparable commodities. Couturiers protect the identity of true believers willing to pay £100,000 for a single haute couture dress while peppering the front row with celebrities such as Nicole Kidman, Oprah Winfrey and Madonna to promote the label and occasionally loan stock models.

Following this pattern, Savile Row may retain its aura of a gentleman's club rather than a fashion boutique. The Row still survives and thrives on "by appointment" custom and absolute discretion that is a precious commodity in a world that wants to know who cuts P. Diddy's suits or where David Beckham buys his underpants. Both Henry Poole & Co. and Anderson & Sheppard were famed in the Edwardian era for demanding at least two letters of introduction from reliable customers before their doors were opened to a new boy.

Like doctors, they would never divulge the identity of their bespoke customers, literally until death. Many men still consider it vulgar when asked to name their tailor. "Who's suit are you wearing?" should always be answered with a smug "Mine." But this doesn't prevent Savile Row taking a leaf out of haute couture's book and using the odd "profile client," as Carlo Brandelli calls celebrities, in order to protect the men who pay full price for their bespoke suits. Richard James has been smart to allow "professional clients" such as British *GQ* editor Dylan Jones to serve as walking billboards for his bespoke suits while resisting the urge to namedrop private clients. As James says, "when a customer wears his first bespoke suit I want the reaction to be that he looks younger, fitter and hotter. What they don't want is someone saying 'great Richard James suit.' The man wears the suit and not vice versa."

Made-to-measure and ready-to-wear services are an inevitable reality for many of the bespoke tailors for bottom lines and headlines. The fashion press cannot photograph bespoke unless the houses are prepared to make "stock" that will fit a standard model size. In the fifties, sixties and seventies, Savile Row did produce annual press collections presented in a catwalk format.

Realistically, a pure bespoke business will be a small business. Both Poole and Dege & Skinner operate licensing agreements for ready-to-wear with Japan, and there is not one Savile Row tailor who will deny that the USA market, rather than British custom, has supported the bespoke business since the twenties. In Maurice Sedwell and Jsen Wintle's case, Russia is swiftly becoming the emerging market to challenge the USA as British bespoke suiting's biggest customer. Progressive companies such as Gieves & Hawkes, Ozwald Boateng and Spencer Hart have taken the fight onto international catwalks. Gieves, designed by Joe Casely-Hayford, has shown on the Paris runway, where Nick Hart's eponymous label has also shown, for the last three seasons. Boateng has shown in Milan for years, and was invited by Pitti Uomo to show a collection of short films he has directed about his collections in the Palazzo Antinori. Boateng also led Givenchy Homme's ready-to-wear operation from Paris. Richard James, Timothy Everest, Hardy Amies and Kilgour's ready-to-wear make regular appearances in the international men's glossies such as *GQ Style*, *L'Uomo Vogue*, *Fashion Inc* and *Vogue Hommes International*.

All Savile Row bespoke tailors are accustomed to regular overseas trips to the USA, Middle East and Japan. Brian Lishak recalls the parties aboard the Queen Mary when Savile Row decamped to New York. Tommy Nutter's one-time partner Edward Sexton did as much business on the dance floor of Studio 54 as he ever did on the Row. "Whatever I wore, they ordered," he says, "from Jerry Zipkin to Bill Blass." When an Eastern potentate places a sufficiently extravagant order, his tailor could practically take the rest of the year off in Barbados on the proceeds.

But however international Savile Row's outlook may be, the unique selling point of the street is its longevity. The square mile that contains Savile Row, Jermyn Street and St. James's Street forms an axis of bespoke gentleman's requisites that has survived since Beau

Brummell's glory days at the turn of the nineteenth century. This corner of London remains a man's world where the great gentleman's clubs of St. James's like White's and The Athenaeum still bridle at the thought of lady members. The order books of vintners (Berry Bros. & Rudd), shirt makers (Turnbull & Asser), hatters (Lock) and shoemakers (Cleverley and Lobb) can match Savile Row name for illustrious name.

The very district where these businesses can be found—Piccadilly— was named for the makers of ruffs, or "pickadils," in the Elizabethan era. Is there any other quarter in any other city in the world that can lay claim to customers such as Emperor Napoleon III, Tsars of Russia, Kings of England and every other crowned head in Europe? Savile Row has dressed the last four Princes of Wales (George IV, Edward VII, the Duke of Windsor and Prince Charles), all of whom were figureheads for the Row, as are many of the world's surviving crowned heads.

Silver screen idols that only need one name for instant recognition were all dressed on the Row including Valentino, Fairbanks, Gable, Astaire, Cooper, Olivier, Coward and Dietrich. Fast-forwarding to the twenty-first century we see contemporary leaders of fashion like Paul Bettany, Daniel Craig, Jude Law and David Beckham all wearing Savile Row bespoke. Designers who were trained on the Row include Alexander McQueen (Anderson & Sheppard) and Stella McCartney (Edward Sexton and Henry Rose, who now trades above McCartney's Bruton Street shop).

Savile Row's story is ultimately the survival of the fittest. Some of the Row's most famous names, like the legendary Scholte who dressed the dapper Duke of Windsor, are no more. Though his heirs went on to found Anderson & Sheppard. Others like Maurice Sedwell thrive under visionary *protégés* like current guv'nor Andrew Ramroop who executes some of the most innovative work on the Row while trading under his late mentor's name. Or take Alan Bennett and Malcolm Plews, who took the helm at two of the oldest firms on the Row, Davies & Son and Welsh & Jeffries. Bennett is a formidable guv'nor while Plews is acknowledged as one of the greatest cutters on the Row.

Arguably the greatest resurrection on the Row is Anderson &

Sheppard. The firm was forced out of its Savile Row address and relocated to Old Burlington Street (parallel to the Row), consequently moving from strength to strength. Owned by the late newspaper magnate Mr. Tiny Rowland, the firm has found a new lease of life under the direction of MD Mr. John Hitchcock and Rowland's daughter Anda, who has become a cornerstone of Savile Row Bespoke and a great spokeswoman for a company infamous for its refusal to address, let alone dress, the press. Houses such as Henry Poole & Co. and Dege & Skinner are similarly being passed to the new generation with the chairmen's sons Simon Cundey and William Skinner assuming responsibility for the firms' futures.

Renewal is a sentiment members of Savile Row Bespoke heartily endorse. A Savile Row bespoke suit remains a marker of success and affluence that London's (if not the world's) new money—from Mayfair hedge funds to city bankers, Middle-Eastern potentates or sybaritic Russians—all aspire to. Savile Row is almost permanently gridlocked today with new Bentleys, Jaguars, Porsches and Rolls-Royces finessing the street's draconian parking arrangements to step from the street to their tailors' doorsteps.

Surrounded by smart restaurants such as Sartoria and Cecconi's, where it's not uncommon to see men in black tie propping-up the bar, Savile Row is once again a glamorous destination where it pays to dress your best. Do try wearing the London Cut and a sharp tie in Mayfair and you'll notice how charming maitre d's from Claridge's to The Wolesley will be. As Huntsman MD David Coleridge concedes, "the suit worn with an open-necked shirt is acceptable now on the Row but I think that comes hand-in-hand with the fact that the average age of men and women working on Savile Row is probably closer to 40 than 70."

The perception that Savile Row is a faded Edwardian throwback populated by grey old men in dusty chalk stripe suits as thick as a retiring ambassador's waistline could not be further from the truth. Age is becoming increasingly irrelevant, and Richard James asserts that "my customers could be 16 or 60, but they are increasingly in very good shape and display the London Cut to its best advantage." So what defines the fabled London Cut and sets it apart from Italian or American tailoring? Edward Sexton says "a little more emphasis on the shoulder, a little more expression into the chest area: that's what gives a suit Sexton appeal." It is Sexton who cheekily proclaimed that when the actors he dressed for the movie *Poor Little Rich Girl* (about the doomed heiress Barbara Hutton) put on his suits they got an erection. Huntsman's Peter Smith describes the London Cut as "sharp-shouldered, with a slightly elongated coat and the one-button line that is notoriously difficult to balance" while Welsh & Jeffries' Malcolm Plews sums it up: "if it is bespoken by the customer we can cut it. But we won't send a gentleman out of the shop looking anything less than immaculate."

Suffice it to say that every tailor subtly varies the line. Anderson & Sheppard's "limp look" is closer in spirit to the preppy American Brooks Brothers silhouette, while Tony Lutwyche's cut for Lutwyche Bespoke is "disciplined, traditional but certainly not stiff." Far from being a totem of the tired, old establishment, the London Cut has dash, urgency and swagger that appeal to men who wish to express power, independence and adventurousness. There is a strong argument that the inherent narcissism of spending thousands of pounds on one's appearance makes Savile Row as attractive to men of questionable character as it does to pillars of the establishment.

In the good old bad days, Savile Row extended unlimited credit to the great and the good. Credit was the temporary undoing of Savile Row founding father Henry Poole, who allowed insolvent aristocrats to stretch their credit until it snapped. Historically, the men who paid attention to their clothes were not by and large responsible statesmen or reliable captains of industry. Instead, Savile Row became a haven for dissolute Maharajas, *louche* Sultans, gentleman gamblers and risk takers of the highest order.

The great customers of the Row were invariably infamous instead of famous: the reckless Emperor Napoleon III who began and ended his association with Poole's in exile, feckless Bosie Douglas, Oscar Wilde's lover, the Emperor of Mexico (who was shot by his own people), King Edward VIII, who gave up the throne for the love of Mrs. Simpson (not to mention bespoke suits) and his great-nephew Charles, present Prince of Wales, who divorced Diana, Princess of Wales and after her death married mistress Camilla Parker-Bowles. The great characters that patronize the Row are living proof that being well dressed seldom coincides with being well behaved. Neil "Bunny" Roger, the society dressmaker whose extraordinary wardrobe was auctioned by Sotheby's in 1998, was sent down from Balliol for homosexual practices and spent his life surrounded by a set Evelyn Waugh described as "lesbians, tarts and joy boys." Dressed by Watson, Fargerstrom & Hughes, Roger dressed in what can only be described as the neo-Edwardian line spiced with a circus pony's color sense. *Vogue USA*'s European editor Hamish Bowles famously bought several of Rogers' suits and starved himself into their twenty-eight-inch waists.

Alan Bennett of Davies & Son recalls seeing Roger tripping down Savile Row in a canary yellow two-piece and tall coke (bowler) hat on his way to visit Sir Hardy Amies, a prolific customer of the street he shared with bespoke tailors. Until his recent illness, Mount Street tailor Douglas Hayward dressed the most glamorous men in the world including Michael Caine for the iconic fashion film *The Italian Job*. His parties were legendary on the Row and, by all accounts, Hayward was one of the most amusing men in London.

Today's most notorious "joy boy" bespoke customer is the artist and "divine dandy" Sebastian Horsley, who was famously crucified in the Philippines; an event that was filmed by Sarah Lucas and shown at the Institute of Contemporary Arts, London. Horsley, whose autobiography *Dandy in the Underworld* is to be published this year, spent the millions he gathered in his twenties speculating on the stock market on Savile Row bespoke suits cut by Richard Anderson and Soho tailors Mark Powell and John Pearse.

A reformed junkie and male escort who is a connoisseur of courtesans and lives opposite John Pearse's shop on Meard Street, Horsley requested John Pearse fashion a holster of "pen pockets" inside his suit jackets that were loaded-up nightly with syringes of heroin and crack cocaine. Currently under construction at Richard Anderson are two cocktail suits cut respectively from red and black sequined cloth. Though all of the Savile Row bespoke tailors are included in the following pages of *The London Cut*, we give you a taste of the Row's priceless history that can only be satisfied by becoming a lifelong visitor. You may, in time, discover which Savile Row tailor was fitting a senior member of the Royal family in the private apartments of Buckingham Palace only to spy Ozwald Boateng below performing for the cameras in the palace courtyard as he received his O.B.E. You may be privileged to discover which British retail tycoon placed a large order on the Row only to reject the finished article when they failed to make him any less porcine than he actually is.

Savile Row endures because and not despite of its reputation as the tailor to some of the world's most notorious and celebrated men. *The London Cut* reflects the dissolute and distinguished customers who have walked through Savile Row bespoke tailors' doors over the past two centuries and considers the past, present and future for Savile Row.

For the present, it is my great privilege to introduce you to the master tailors of Savile Row.

Thursday, November 9, 2006, London

THE FOUNDERS

ANDERSON & SHEPPARD: THE HOLLYWOOD CONNECTION

HISTORY

Founded in 1906, Anderson & Sheppard coincided roughly with the birth of the motion picture industry in Hollywood. Both would be propelled to a pinnacle of glamour and sophistication during the roaring twenties. The firm can trace its bloodline directly to a true Savile Row legend: fiery, flame-haired Dutchman Mr. Scholte. Prior to WWI, Scholte was head cutter at military tailor Johns & Pegg and dressed George V's brother-in-law Lord Athlone. Squaring up opposite Henry Poole on the Row, Scholte revolutionized civilian tailoring by stealing tricks from the dynamic of military tunics. *Tailor and Cutter* christened his soft-shouldered lounge suits the "London Cut": the venerable journal of the trade.

The Prince of Wales (later the Duke of Windsor) was Scholte's most famous disciple and there's a popular tale of Scholte making the Prince a black morning coat overnight after an outraged George V condemned his son for wearing grey to Royal Ascot. Per Anderson was a Swedish-born striker (under cutter) for Scholte who was taught the London Cut by the master. In 1906, Per set up

Anderson & Simmons on Sackville Street but his partner Simmons emigrated to South Africa in 1909.

Simmons' sister was married to a chap named Sidney Horatio Sheppard who was trained at Tautz as a breeches maker. SHS invested £2,000 in the business and by 1913 Anderson & Sheppard was born at no. 13 Savile Row. Anderson staffed the firm with fellow Swedes who were adept at the "limp look." By 1928 Anderson & Sheppard had expanded into 30 Savile Row and increased production by 100%. According to *The Savile Row Story*, Scholte meanwhile went into a familiar decline. "The great man's sons were more interested in wearing clothes than in making them . . . the client list was plundered by staff . . . Scholte died rich and that was the end." It was the snobbery of Scholte and another of the Prince's tailors, Hawes & Curtis, that delivered Savile Row icon Fred Astaire to Anderson & Sheppard's door.

Astaire was already a star in the thirties when he met the Prince of Wales backstage after a West End engagement. No stranger to blue bloods, Astaire's sister and former dancing partner Adele was married into the Duke of Devonshire's family. Astaire appraised "the best dressed young man in the world" and appreciated the cut of the Prince's lapels and the fact that the white waistcoat did not show beneath his dress coat front.

When Astaire went to Hawes & Curtis the next day, the firm snootily regretted that they could not recreate the Prince's white tie and tails for Mr. Astaire (who was, after all, in show business). But Anderson & Sheppard obliged. Worn by Astaire, Andersons' top hat, white tie and tails was an example of Savile Row poetry in motion that has proved timeless.

Anderson & Sheppard were not strangers to the silver screen. Rudolph Valentino had been a customer before his death in 1926 but seeing as his enduring image was that of the sheikh, his on-screen wardrobe was hardly the ringing endorsement for the Row that Astaire became. But the following generation of English imports to Hollywood—Jack Buchanan, Ronald Coleman, Leslie Howard, Noel Coward, Cary Grant and anglophile Gary Cooper—all exported Savile Row style to a USA audience. Clifton Webb was sufficiently moved by an Anderson & Sheppard suit to declare "In a word, English tailors make clothes for gentlemen." USA tough guy movie stars Bogart, Gable and Cagney may have popularized the coat hanger silhouette, but frankly this mobster shoulder looked better on Joan Crawford than James Cagney.

Hollywood patronage was occasionally a double-edged sword. Crooner Bing Crosby recalled an appointment at Lesley & Roberts that ended in the "degradation and shame" of a moth flying out of a long-neglected bolt of cloth. At the height of its fame the six story Lesley & Roberts building was known as "the lighthouse" because its windows blazed through the night to keep up with demand. The firm did not survive Crosby's remark.

Meanwhile, Anderson & Sheppard was moving up in the world. Sir Waldron Sinclair, a friend of Sidney Horatio Sheppard, became chairman in the twenties. Anderson & Sheppard stalwart Mr. Halsey recalls "How Sheppard ever became a tailor I do not know . . . He was extremely autocratic and he never mixed with other tailors." Mr. Halsey continues: "In those days we had a proper boardroom on the first floor and the board meeting was something to behold: half a dozen Rolls-Royces lined up in Savile Row with their liveried attendants awaiting their lords and masters."

The company's reputation for not mixing with the Row was established from the beginning. Anderson & Sheppard's highhanded attitude certainly irked *The Savile Row Story* author Richard Walker, who sniped that the firm was "secretive and hidebound by tradition even though (it didn't have) a particularly aristocratic clientele. Shunning publicity, it consequently gets a lot." Walker was writing in 1988 when Anderson & Sheppard was the most successful Savile Row bespoke tailor until well into the 1980s "for all its irritating aloofness." With the benefit of hindsight, perhaps it was because of aloofness that the firm prospered.

Anderson & Sheppard had good reason to feel superior. As Mr. Halsey recalls after the abdication crisis in 1937, "the great dandies from Italy, Spain, South America and Romania beat a path to no. 30. Major E.D. "Fruity" Metcalfe (the Duke of Windsor's equerry) was an Anderson & Sheppard client of long standing and said—within my hearing—to Sidney Horatio Sheppard 'I shall bring the Duke in very soon' to which the old man replied 'I shall esteem it a great favor if

you do not do that, sir.' Sheppard, I think wisely, did not want
anything to do with British royalty."
Anderson & Sheppard excelled at dressing Hollywood royalty rather
than the ever-dwindling European royal houses. Their clients were
discreet but very flamboyant men such as Senator Benton (who
owned Encyclopædia Britannica) who only ever wore white suits:
cashmere in winter, cotton in summer. Douglas Fairbanks Sr.
indulged his fetish for overcoats at Anderson & Sheppard while
Henry Ford II ordered thirty-five cashmere jackets in less than seven
minutes. The Maharajah of Alwar was, according to Halsey, the
house's most prolific client and comparable in wealth to Bill Gates
or the Sultan of Brunei today.
Long forgotten Anderson & Sheppard eccentrics include the South
American speculator José Chopitea, who never ordered less than fifty
suits a year to be sent to Avenida El Rosario, Lima, Peru. Chopitea's
valet, in town to buy his master 200 Sulka silk ties, told Mr. Halsey
that he had a very large house built to house his Savile Row suits.
Mistakes in Mr. Halsey's experience included opening a Paris branch
of Anderson & Sheppard only shortly before Hitler came to town, and
opening a city branch when "the amount of business brains in
Anderson & Sheppard at the time wouldn't fill a thimble."
Anderson & Sheppard had a good war (WWII) with Arthur
Lockwood, a *protégé* of Scholte, running the shop because he was too
old for military service. The clothing coupon problem didn't apply to
foreign nationals and this suited Anderson & Sheppard fine thanks to
its mighty business stateside. Anderson & Sheppard were fortunate to
end the war untouched by the Blitz unlike Gieves, J. Dege & Sons,
Meyer & Mortimer and Pope & Bradbury who all suffered direct hits.
Anderson & Sheppard never seemed to have noticed the world
changing around it as the fifties boom times turned into the
swinging sixties and the eighties designer suit era closed many of the
company's bespoke peers. In 1988 Condé Nast *Traveller* journalist
Simon Winchester infiltrated Anderson & Sheppard the only way he
knew how: by becoming a bespoke customer. He paints a vivid
picture of shop manager Mr. Dennis Hallbery in his heyday.
"I was taken into a fitting room as large as most small houses and
with mirrors that might have graced the main staircase of a Palladian

House. Five men deployed themselves to battle stations . . . Mr. Hallbery twirled around me, measuring, barking numbers . . . 'Some folks swear by our coat. Others swear at them. It's an old joke. But it's quite true. You'll see. You'll want double-breasted of course. No pocket flaps. Four-button cuffs. Perfectly normal, perfectly classic.'" Hallbery's behavior was anything but remarkable on the Row at that time.

Anderson & Sheppard's famous shop on the corner of Savile Row and Clifford Street (no. 30) seemed immune to the changing social climate. By January 1987 the company was listed under Volga Investments (offshore in Jersey) and its chairman was listed as Josie Rowland (wife of media mogul Tiny Rowland). Of its £1,540,000 turnover, it made a pretax profit of £318,000 with almost two-thirds of its revenue generated in the USA. Needless to say, the 1987 New York Stock Market crash shook the firm to its foundations. But Richard James still distinctly remembers the blinds being drawn at 5 p.m. and any customer who arrived a whisker past the hour was denied admission.

THE COMPANY TODAY

In 2005 Anderson & Sheppard's landlords forced the company to leave no. 30 Savile Row and relocate behind Queensbury House at 32 Old Burlington Street. Light, bright and welcoming, Anderson & Sheppard under MD Mr. John Hitchcock and guv'nor's daughter Anda Rowland is transformed. The business was attractive enough to interest USA fashion magnates Calvin Klein and Ralph Lauren, who offered five million dollars to acquire the company from the Rowland family and, after being turned down, founded his Purple Label made-to-measure tailoring division inspired by his adventures on Savile Row.

Another fashion icon bewitched by Anderson & Sheppard bespoke is Tom Ford, who is also opening his own top-drawer made-to-measure tailoring business in association with Ermenegildo Zegna. Anda Rowland has done more to modernize Anderson & Sheppard in the last year than this superior company has attempted in a century. MD Mr. Hitchcock steered the company smoothly from the old address to its new abode and nobody jumped ship during the journey.

Respectful of the house's refusal to dilute their purely bespoke service, Sheppard is a leading light of Savile Row Bespoke. She is currently negotiating an event in conjunction with he Chambre Syndicale de la Haute Couture to show Savile Row bespoke in Paris during Couture week. Meanwhile, a newly optimistic Anderson & Sheppard is welcoming a new generation of glamorous international playboys and entrepreneurs into this clubhouse for twenty-first century dandies.

HOUSE STYLE

You either love or hate Anderson & Sheppard's "limp look" silhouette of softly tailored jackets that drape the body beneath rather than build the illusion of a shape that doesn't exist. Anderson & Sheppard's signature cut hasn't changed since the days of Clifton Webb, who described it thus: "The shoulders are wider and have less padding, an attempt is made to create a recognizable waistline, there's a better fit around the hips and the sleeves are slimmer."

FAMOUS/INFAMOUS CUSTOMERS

Rudolph Valentino, Charlie Chaplin, Douglas Fairbanks Sr., the Maharajah of Alwar, Fred Astaire, Major E.D. "Fruity" Metcalfe, Diaghilev, Leonide Massine, Alec & Evelyn Waugh, Somerset Maugham, Ralph Richardson, Sir Sacheverall Sitwell, Marlene Dietrich, Gary Cooper, Sir Noel Coward, Sir Laurence Olivier, Kirk Douglas, George Segal, Samuel Goldwyn, Hon. Averill Harriman, Buster Keaton, Duke Ellington, Oscar Peterson, Sir John Betjeman, Otto Preminger, Rudolph Nureyev, Sir Alec Guinness, H.R.H. Prince Charles, Manolo Blahnik, Ralph Fiennes, Ralph Lauren, Calvin Klein, Tom Ford.

ADDRESS

ANDERSON & SHEPPARD, 32 Old Burlington Street, London W1S 3AT. Tel. +44 207 245 0594. www.anderson-sheppard.co.uk

BY APPOINTMENT
TO H.R.H. THE DUKE OF EDINBURGH
MILITARY TAILORS
JOHNS & PEGG

Davies & Son

Incorporating

JOHNS & PEGG *Wells* *James & James*

38 Savile Row, London W1S 3QE

www.savilerow.uk.com

Telephone: 020 7434 3016, 020 7734 1713 & 020 7734 1748   Fax: 020 7287 4348

www.daviesandson.com

e-mail: davandson@aol.com

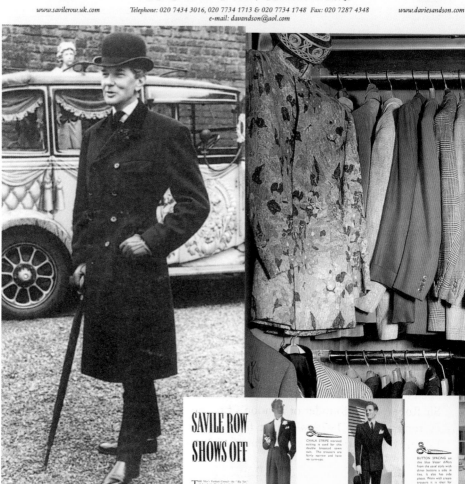

SAVILE ROW SHOWS OFF

DAVIES & SON:
THE PROTECTOR

HISTORY

Davies & Son stakes its claim as the oldest independent tailor in and around the Row. Thomas Davies inherited the Cork Street tailoring business left by his deceased brother and moved to Hanover Street in 1804. Before inheriting the business, Thomas Davies worked for Greenwalls, procurement agents for the Royal Navy, and Davies boasted tailoring for the famous sailor of the age: Admiral Lord Nelson, whose victory at Trafalgar led to a buoyant naval officer class keen to order their uniforms and civilian suits at their leader's bespoke tailor. During Thomas Davies's tenure as guv'nor, Davies & Son claimed to dress "all the crowned heads of Europe."

Sir Robert Peel, founder of London's first police force, was a famous customer and, in 1979 when the firm moved from Hanover Street, a bill of the great man's for the sum of £128 was discovered dated 1829. But one particular uncrowned head in the British royal family unintentionally led the firm into the middle of one of Savile Row's greatest scandals in 1892. In the nineteenth century, labor subcontracted to sweatshops in London by the great houses on and around Savile Row became the focus of unwelcome attention.

Angelica Patience Fraser, "the tailors' Florence Nightingale," began religious readings in these sweatshops in 1875.

In 1880 Miss Fraser called a conference about "sweating" and held a tailors-against-drink rally in response to the notorious "Carnaby Boys": a clique of drunkard tailors working around Soho. A House of Lords inquiry followed and led no less a firm than Henry Poole (an icon of Savile Row then as now) to condemn sweatshop labor. Davies & Son signed a resolution to improve conditions. It was a Ms. Fanny Hicks who, in 1892, told her Trades Union Congress in Glasgow that the Duke of York (later George V) had his trousers made in a sweatshop where she knew fever to have broken out, and told the tribunal that the subcontractor was Davies & Son.

The Duke's brother (heir apparent and grandson of Queen Victoria) Prince Edward, Duke of Clarence, had died suddenly in January 1892 as had the daughter of Davies & Son customer Sir Robert Peel. But the Duke clearly did not lay the scandal or the death of his brother at Davies & Son's door. As King George V, he awarded the firm his Royal Warrant and, according to *The Savile Row Story*, "created a room for his exclusive use (in Hanover Square) and fitted it with panels and a tube like a hose pipe which communicated with the tailors upstairs." George V was as solid a customer of Davies & Son as he was King and introduced his sons to their father's tailor of choice.

Though the Prince of Wales was a famous customer of Scholte, he also patronized Davies & Son and continued to do so when he became King Edward VIII then Duke of Windsor well into the sixties. Incidentally, Scholte sold out to James & James, later bought by Davies & Son. The last Davies exited the firm in 1935 and the firm was taken over by its cutters, who continued to run the firm until 1996. These were glamorous but turbulent times. Davies & Son was swift to capitalize on the Duke of Windsor association, attracting Hollywood royalty such as Clark Gable and Tyrone Power. In 1952 another stellar Davies & Son customer, Douglas Fairbanks Jr., was moved to declare "Savile Row has recaptured the tailoring supremacy of the world."

In 1979, the firm left Hanover Street and George V's private room, taking with it fitting room chairs, fenders, fireplace screens and records rediscovered after a century of neglect. By now 90% of Davies & Son's turnover was international trade. The firm announced, "our business was built on the clothing requirements of the aristocracy of Europe and Great Britain. Today our business is mainly with the affluent and famous abroad; an ideal commercial profile, we are advised, in times when exports are of prime importance."

THE COMPANY TODAY
Alan Bennett, visionary MD and custodian of Savile Row's history, bought Davies & Son in 1997. Bennett trained under Dege & Skinner MD Michael Skinner and has over forty years' experience in bespoke tailoring. Davies & Son had already incorporated Bostridge & Curties and Watson, Fargerstrom & Hughes (Bunny Roger's tailor), but Bennett went on to add great bespoke tailoring houses Johns & Pegg (the nineteenth century royal, military and household cavalry tailor), James & James (who had acquired Scholte when the great man retired) and Wells of Mayfair (established on Maddox Street in 1829). Bennett had his name above the door on Savile Row in the late eighties servicing his own book of "businessmen, stockbrokers, a few Lords, Earls . . . " He gained a reputation as a tailor to the court of St. James's overseas ambassadors and continues to tailor for High Commissioners in the remaining British colonies. Today, Davies & Son on Savile Row is the only "old school" bespoke tailoring house left on the west side of the Row. This important name still attracts the great and the good of the British establishment.

HOUSE STYLE
Masters in the "English cut: a combination of style, cutting and craftsmanship essential to creating the look that flatters the figure and communicates substance. A waisted jacket, straight shoulder and egg-shaped armhole evolved from the military riding coats of the past."

ROYAL WARRANTS
H.R.H. the Duke of Edinburgh (military tailors).

FAMOUS/INFAMOUS CUSTOMERS

Admiral Lord Nelson, Sir Robert Peel, George V, the Maharajah of Cooch Behar, the Duke of Windsor, H.R.H. the Duke of Edinburgh, Ambassador Joseph Kennedy (father of JFK), Douglas Fairbanks Jr., Sir Oswald Mosely, Colonel Edward Boxshall (British spy chief), Lord Alexander of Tunis, Field Marshall Douglas Haig, President Harry Truman, Benny Goodman, Irving Berlin, Clark Gable, Tyrone Power, Bing Crosby, Calvin Klein, Michael Jackson, John Frieda.

ADDRESS

DAVIES & SON, 38 Savile Row, London W1S 3QE. Tel. +44 207 434 3016. www.daviesandsonsavilerow.com

ROYAL STABLES
Mess Dress

ROYAL OMAN POLICE, MOUNTED PIPE BAND
PRELIMINARY DESIGNS

DEGE & SKINNER:
MILITARY PRECISION

HISTORY

The Dege & Skinner families' personal and professional lives have
intertwined since 1880, even though the names did not unite on
Savile Row until 2000 under present chairman Mr. Michael
Skinner and his son (managing director) William. The story began
in 1865 when German immigrant Jacob Dege opened his first
tailor's shop at no. 13 Conduit Street, a stone's throw from Savile
Row and now an office building nestled between Yohji
Yamamoto's London flagship and chi-chi cocktail bar Sketch.
Jacob's youngest son Arthur Dege first encountered William
Skinner at Merchant Taylors' School in 1880. Also a scion of a
London tailoring dynasty, William Skinner's family operated from
57 Jermyn Street (now a private members' club). Dege and
Skinner became firm friends and—in a move that must have
dismayed their parents—partners in Arthur Dege & Skinner which
opened on Grafton Street at the turn of the twentieth century. The
death of Arthur's older brothers prompted his return into the
family fold in 1910 (the year Edward VII died) and the name

Dege & Skinner would not appear above a West End tailor's shop for another ninety years.

William Skinner died in 1912 following a riding accident in Richmond Park and, in a Dickensian gesture, old Jacob Dege took Skinner's two sons under his wing. One of them, William Skinner Junior (or Tim as he became known), entered J. Dege & Sons in 1916. He was the present chairman's father. Anti-German sentiment during World War I forced Jacob Dege to resign the chairmanship of the firm in 1917. Wealthy but embittered, he became exiled to his country estate in Balcombe and died a year later.

The depression in the thirties and the onset of World War II erased memories of bespoke tailoring's golden Edwardian era and in 1941 Tim Skinner, now MD of the firm under the receiver, arrived at work only to find no. 13 Conduit Street bombed flat. J. Dege & Sons moved to 10 Clifford Street, sharing the premises with Perkins, Sandon & Hepburn (an arrangement not uncommon on Savile Row today). J. Dege & Sons survived the war providing uniforms infinitely less glamorous than the masterpieces they traditionally made for dashing Edwardian cavalry officers. The Skinner family bought J. Dege & Sons in 1947 and founder Jacob Dege's grandson John rejoined the firm following his military service.

In 1951 J. Dege & Sons moved back to Conduit Street (on the site now occupied by the The Westbury Hotel's Polo Bar) and purchased two revered tailoring houses (J. Daniels & Co. and George B. Winter and Tracy). The house had already acquired, in 1939, Wilkinson & Son (founded in 1839) the tailor and robe maker by appointment to every monarch since Queen Victoria. The investment in Wilkinson & Son paid dividends in 1953 when H.M. Queen Elizabeth II was crowned, and demand for court dress, peers' robes and diplomatic uniforms peaked.

The coronation was Michael Skinner's introduction to the family firm, and he was the first to recognize a future for J. Dege & Sons beyond Mayfair. He initiated Dege's regular visits to the USA in 1964, and as an avid horseman who completed the Badminton Horse Trials in 1961, he was great advertisement for Dege's riding and hunting attire. The acquisition of Rogers, John Jones military tailors in 1967 tripled the size of J. Dege & Sons overnight. The prestigious

Rogers, established in 1774, was the famed military tailor to the Cavalry and Guards while John Jones (1827) was an army clothier and contractor who made his name during the Crimean War. Through John Jones, J. Dege & Sons also inherited the international club color specialists Foster & Co. (founded in 1840).

In 1973 when Princess Anne first married, her husband Captain Mark Phillips was resplendent in the scarlet tunic of the First Queen's Dragoon Guards made by J. Dege & Sons. Photographed for *Vogue* by Lord Litchfield, Capt. Mark Phillips evoked the glory days of empire and breathtaking bespoke military uniforms. With the only British Royal wedding of the decade as a shop window, Michael Skinner followed his first visit to Japan with the first of many visits to the Sultanate of Oman in 1977. In 1981 H.M. Sultan Qaboos conferred the first of an exotic trio of Royal Warrants on J. Dege & Sons; the others came in 1984 courtesy of H.M. the Queen in recognition of the firm's work on state uniforms for the Quincentenary of the Queen's Body Guard of the Yeoman of the Guard, and H.M. the King of Bahrain who signed his Royal Warrant at Riffa Palace in the presence of chairman Skinner in 2003.

THE COMPANY TODAY

In 1989 J. Dege & Sons moved to its present address at no. 10 Savile Row and acquired Helman, tailor by appointment to H.R.H. Prins Bertil of Sweden and winner of two *Tailor & Cutter* "Dandy" awards. In 2000, Michael Skinner renamed the company Dege & Skinner and in the same year was elected president of the Royal Warrant Holders Association. His son William Skinner, who joined the company in 1993, is now managing director of the firm and responsible for the company's regular overseas visits to the USA, Middle East and Far East. The company has licensed in Japan since 1977. Dege & Skinner was the first Savile Row bespoke tailor to have its own bespoke shirt maker on the premises in the person of Mr. Robert Whittaker, who joined the firm in 1994. John, the last Dege to work in the family firm, died in 2000 after having retired in 1988. 2005 was the 140th anniversary of the firm's foundation and Michael Skinner, as Master of the Worshipful Company of

Merchant Taylors (founded in 1327) reintroduced white tie with decorations to the guild's annual banquet for the Lord Mayor of the City of London. In 2007 Michael Skinner remains chairman of Dege & Skinner and though technically retired, his presence is still felt at meetings of Savile Row Bespoke, of which he is a founder member.

HOUSE STYLE
One can practically hear the national anthem on entering Dege & Skinner. Equestrians, military men and monarchs need have no fear even though lesser mortals may be a little intimidated by the old school and regimental ties on display. But persist. While shirt maker Robert Whittaker quietly cuts his cloth beneath a proud photograph of Princess Anne and Captain Mark Phillips on their wedding day (the Princess has since remarried), you begin to see touches of the exotic in the shop like an illustration of Sultan Qaboos's Royal Oman Police Camel Pipe Band regalia designed by Dege & Skinner or the splendid new Royal Warrant of Bahrain's King Hamad. Not for nothing was Gianni Versace's last bespoke order placed at Dege & Skinner.

The firm's expertise as a military tailor is proudly displayed throughout the shop and it is Dege & Skinner's military precision that gives the house its unique flavor. Like all Savile Row houses, Dege & Skinner can make whatever the customer has "bespoken," but let Dege & Skinner use some of the tailoring techniques learnt on the parade ground to cut a dashing city or evening suit. For country clothes—hunting, shooting or simply weekending at Chatsworth—Dege & Skinner is unsurpassed. The house woven silk tie incorporating Dege & Skinner's leaping fox emblem will gain you instant respect at the Badminton or Burghley Horse Trials where Dege & Skinner annually present a bespoke riding coat to the best British rider under 25 who has not yet won full international honors. In 2004, this was won by Zara Phillips, daughter of Princess Anne and Captain Mark Phillips.

PRESENT ROYAL WARRANTS
H.M. the Queen, H.M. the Sultan of Oman, H.M. the King of Bahrain.

FAMOUS/INFAMOUS CUSTOMERS
George Bush Sr., Prins Bertil of Sweden, Captain Mark Phillips, Joanna Lumley,

Colin Montgomerie, Michael Jackson, David Bowie, Egon Ronay, Gianni Versace; former Helman customers include Lord Rothschild and Lord Hanson.

ADDRESS

DEGE & SKINNER, 10 Savile Row, London W1S 3PF. Tel. +44 207 287 2941.
www.dege-skinner.co.uk

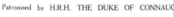

EDE & RAVENSCROFT:
A DUTY TO SERVE

HISTORY
Ede & Ravenscroft may have an imposing presence at the top of
Savile Row today (at no. 8 Burlington Gardens) but its true heart lies
in Chancery Lane, surrounded by the old City of London's Inns of
Court. The grand old man of robe making and tailoring was
established in 1689, the year of William & Mary's coronation. The
firm has held successive Royal Warrants as robe makers to every
monarch from George III to our present Queen.
In 1689 neither Ede nor Ravenscroft's name was above the door of
the company. Founded by the Shudall family, the firm passed into
the hands of Mr. William Webb who, in 1797, advertised his
expertise as "maker of robes for peers, peeresses & bishops,
coronation, installation, judges, sergeants, clergymen, King's council,
barristers and attorneys, livery gowns and robes for any corporation of
Great Britain." 1821 was Webb's finest hour when George IV was
crowned in particularly overwrought pomp after enduring years of
Regency deputizing for his "mad" father George III.
Joseph Ede is first recorded as Webb's apprentice in 1811 and,

though Webb's son Frederick assumed the mantle of royal robe maker after his father's death, he went on to sell the business. The buyer? None other than Joseph Ede's uncle Thomas Adams, who acquired the business for his favorite nephew to manage. He rechristened the business Adams & Ede (a terrific biblical pun but for a single letter "d").

Within four years Joseph Ede won Queen Victoria's Royal Warrant. This took place at the beginning of an epoch during which court, state, church and the legal professions were all at their most draconian and elaborately dressed. Joseph saw the first decade of the new Queen's reign before dying and leaving Adams & Ede to his widow Anne. Only 16 at the time, his son Joseph Webb Ede was already in the family firm and took the reigns from his mother in 1869, naming it Ede & Son.

Now begins an intriguing period of the company's history that challenges the assumption that robe making and tailoring was a man's world. Joseph Webb Ede had married Rosanna Ravenscroft in 1871, a scion of the wig-making dynasty founded in 1726 that had serviced Prime Ministers Robert Peel and H.J.H. Asquith and the Duke of Wellington. Six months later Joseph was dead aged only 26. Rosanna, or Rosa Ede as she became known, took the director's chair and held it for a further sixty years, paying homage to her late husband by calling the company Ede, Son & Ravenscroft. Only in 1921 was the "son" dropped and the firm became Ede & Ravenscroft.

Rosa Ede applied for and held Queen Victoria's Royal Warrant until the Queen died in 1901. In her lifetime Rosa's firm made coronation robes for Edward VII and Queen Alexandra (later modified for George V and Queen Mary), the Prince of Wales (later Duke of Windsor), the Duke and Duchess of York (later George VI and Queen Elizabeth), Princess Mary (then Princess Royal), the Duke of Gloucester and Prince George (the "Lost Prince," son of George and Mary who died tragically young hidden from family and nation alike due to his mental illness).

A framed print of Queen Alexandra, signed for Rosa Ede, still hangs in the Chancery Lane shop. For her coronation in 1952, Ede & Ravenscroft was commanded by H.M. Queen Elizabeth II to create "a six-yard train in the best quality handmade purple silk velvet trimmed with the best quality Canadian ermine five inches on top and underside and fully lined with pure silk English satin complete with ermine cape and all being tailed ermine in the traditional manner and including embroidery by the Royal School of Needlework."

THE COMPANY TODAY

Ede & Ravenscroft Chancery Lane continues to act as guardian of both hereditary and life peers' coronation robes. The company continues to fashion robes for new members of the Order of the Garter to wear annually at the Windsor Castle Garter Ceremony. The annual State Opening of Parliament is practically a shop window for Ede & Ravenscroft's craft as it is still attended by the Queen, the peerage, the judiciary and the clergy. The great offices of state, the Earl Marshall (the Duke of Norfolk) and the Lord Great Chamberlain (the Marquees of Cholmondeley) attend wearing the traditional scarlet and gold levee dress worn by their late fathers but remade for the present incumbents. Chancery Lane is also the headquarters from which Ede & Ravenscroft continue to robe the British judiciary and increasingly Commonwealth countries and former colonies. With shops in Oxford and Cambridge, Ede & Ravenscroft retains its supremacy as robe maker to universities.

HOUSE STYLE

Ede & Ravenscroft's elegant outpost at the top of Savile Row declares the company's status and skill as a bespoke tailor of the surviving British establishment dress codes (white tie, black tie and morning coats). Though only the last is acceptable attire for a British wedding, all three are now common currency at weddings worldwide. Ede & Ravenscroft is arguably the only tailor in London that can dress a man in immaculate white tie from the crown of his antique black silk top hat to the tip of his black patent leather lace-up with bespoke, made-to-measure or off-the-peg service. And what service! A chap is treated like a duke even if he's on a pit stop shop for one of Ede & Ravenscroft's rather cool travel or cocktail suits off-the-peg.

ROYAL WARRANTS

H.M. Queen Elizabeth II (robe makers), H.R.H. the Duke of Edinburgh (robe makers), H.M. Queen Elizabeth the Queen Mother (robe makers), H.R.H. Prince of Wales (robe makers).

FAMOUS/INFAMOUS CUSTOMERS

Emperors Napoleon III of France, Alexander III of Russia and Frederick of Prussia; former Kings of Denmark, the Hellenes, Italy, Sweden, Spain and the Netherlands; the Right Hon. Bernard Weatherill (former Speaker of the House of Commons), Baroness Thatcher, the Most Hon. the Marquees of Cholmondeley, the Duke of Norfolk, the Earl of Litchfield.

ADDRESS

EDE & RAVENSCROFT, 8 Burlington Gardens, London, W1X 1LG. Tel. +44 207 734 5450. www.edeandravenscroft.co.uk

GIEVES & HAWKES:
OFFICERS AND GENTLEMEN

HISTORY

Founded respectively in 1785 and 1771, the tailoring houses of
Gieves and Hawkes only merged in 1974, although Hawkes had been
in residence at their current address no. 1 Savile Row since 1912.
Though Hawkes is senior in age, its history is more prosaic while the
story of Gieves is interwoven with the fabric of the British nation.
Stourbridge-born Thomas Hawkes came to London midway through
the eighteenth century to make his fortune. He gained employment
as a journeyman (a runner) for Mr. Moy, a velvet cap maker on
Swallow Street in Soho. As *The Savile Row Story* relates, "Mr. Moy
was 'on the cod'—tailoring slang for drinking heavily—which left
Hawkes plenty of scope to cultivate aristocratic customers."
With a fade-out worthy of an MGM melodrama, the story leaps to
1771 when Hawkes opens his own shop, dresses King George III and
his glamorous son Prinny (the Prince of Wales) and leaves £20,000
when he dies in 1809 at age 64. Hawkes had edged closer to Savile
Row by moving his firm to no. 14 Piccadilly during the last decade
of the eighteenth century. It is tempting to think of Hawkes the

ambitious young entrepreneur ejecting the downward spiraling Mr.
Moy and systematically social climbing with all the alacrity of
a young Ralph Lauren.

As tailor by appointment to the Royal Navy, Gieves had a head start
when founding father "Old Mel" Meredith opened his shop in
Portsmouth in 1785. Britannia had ruled the waves since the armada
in Elizabethan times and in the late eighteenth century the Royal
Navy standardized uniforms . . . rather like the government decreeing
that every man in the city must wear a pinstripe three-piece made by
Henry Poole & Co. Meredith prospered and dressed Admiral Lord
Nelson, who died aboard his flagship H.M.S. Victory resplendent in
heavily braided tunic and breeches at the Battle of Trafalgar in 1805.
The Gieve family patriarch, James Gieve, acquired a partnership with
Mr. Joseph Galt (established in 1823 and incorporating Meredith) in
1852. He rechristened the firm Galt & Gieves in 1852. His equally
ambitious sister Elizabeth earned her own Queen Victoria's Royal
Warrant as dressmaker and milliner (an honor she held until her
retirement in 1889, a year after her brother's death).

James Gieve's son James Watson Gieve doubtless benefited from aunt
Elizabeth's connections with the court. Queen Victoria's grandsons,
Prince Albert Victor (Duke of Clarence) and Prince Edward (later
King George V), were equipped by Gieves for Royal Naval College in
1907 and, later, for their year as Royal Navy Cadets aboard H.M.S.
Britannia. The Windsors' love affair with the sea can be traced back
to "Sailor King" George V who succeeded his father on the arm of his
dead brother Albert Victor's intended (Queen Mary) in 1911 and
gave Gieves his Royal Warrant. The Gieves Sea Chest, patented by
the firm in 1852 for the Crimean War, was mandatory kit at the
Royal Naval College and both King George VI and the Duke of
Windsor owned one as young cadets.

Gieves has held the Royal Warrant ever since. The firm dressed
George V, George VI and the Duke of Windsor when the future
King married Queen Elizabeth the Queen Mother. When the present
Queen and the Duke of Edinburgh wed, Gieves tailored the groom's
uniform. Vice chairman Mr. Robert Gieve, the present patriarch of
Gieves & Hawkes, recalls accompanying "the man from Gieves" to
Buckingham Palace at the age of 11 to fit George VI. He noted the

"easy rapport between the man from Gieves and His Majesty."
It was the first of many visits to the Palace for Robert Gieve, whose
firm went on to dress the Queen, the Duke of Edinburgh, the
Princess Royal, the Duke of York, the Duke of Gloucester, Prince
Michael of Kent, Diana Princess of Wales and her sons the Princes
William & Harry. Indeed, Mr. Gieve's family firm created uniforms
for the weddings of the Prince and Princess of Wales in 1981 and the
Duke and Duchess of York in 1985.

Meanwhile, Hawkes & Co. had acquired no. 1 Savile Row from the
Royal Geographical Society in 1912. A house had stood on the site
since 1732 and had been occupied at one time by Lord George
Cavendish, who commissioned the building of the Burlington Arcade
in 1819. It was recorded that Beau Brummell had been a dinner
guest of George Cavendish and that the famous explorers H.M.
Stanley and David Livingstone had lectured there at the Royal
Geographical Society. Incidentally, when Stanley and Dr. Livingstone
met, the former was dressed by Poole and the latter by Gieves.

Gieves' contribution to WWI and WWII were immense. In 1914,
Gieves patented the Life Saving Waistcoat that came two years too
late for the passengers of the Titanic, but saved thousands of lives
including the present Lord Montagu's father, who survived the
torpedoing of S.S. Persia in 1915. During WWII, Gieves became a
major weapon in the armory of the secret service. Charles Frazer-
Smith (a character not dissimilar to Q in the James Bond films)
commissioned the firm to develop compass buttons, cavity buttons
(concealing explosives, poison pellets and maps printed on silk) and
Gili saws (serrated wire on a ring pull concealed in a cap badge).

As *The Savile Row Story* cleverly puts it, the seventies were unkind
to both Gieves and Hawkes. "A contract from the Imperial Ethiopian
Navy and the enthusiastic personal custom of Emperor Haile Selassie
was small consolation for the loss of so many colonial and dominion
contracts." Nowhere was this more bleakly demonstrated than in
Peru, where Gieves's agent awaited a summons to the Presidential
Palace only to witness a coup that overthrew a potentially lucrative
national contract. Similar losses were felt with revolution in Baghdad
and the deposition of the Greek monarchy. In 1948, officers'
uniforms accounted for 85% of the company's turnover. By 1978 this

was down to 20%. In 1974 Gieves Ltd. made a decision that the present owners must still be thankful for. They acquired Hawkes and the freehold of no. 1 Savile Row, thereby laying the foundations for Gieves & Hawkes' renaissance in the new millennium.

THE COMPANY TODAY

In 2002 Gieves & Hawkes de-listed from the London Stock Exchange and the remaining shares were acquired by majority shareholder Christopher Cheng (US Holdings, Hong Kong). Under new management, Gieves & Hawkes has lived up to its iconic address. Ownership of no. 1 Savile Row makes the company an indestructible cornerstone of bespoke tailoring on the Row. Present managing director Mark Henderson is messianic about "the pinnacle bespoke range while also being very aware that to survive in the twenty-first century Gieves & Hawkes has to roll with the punches and adapt to a constantly evolving men's style market." As chairman of Savile Row Bespoke, he has reignited the collective passions to protect the street and its trade.

Under the watchful eye of Mr. Gary Carr, Gieves & Hawkes continues to operate one of the finest naval and military uniform rooms on the Row. The bespoke rooms are reminiscent of one of the great St. James's Street gentlemen's clubs even though a lady is now one of the firm's star cutters. The royal connection endures as Gieves & Hawkes dressed both Princes William and Harry in immaculate morning coats for the wedding of the Prince of Wales and the Duchess of Cornwall in 2005. A separate shop front at no. 2 Savile Row houses Gieves & Hawkes' fashionable baby brother Gieves. Designed by Joe Casely-Hayford and shown biannually at the Paris collections, Gieves is a young, intelligent and sharp collection that welcomes a new customer onto the Row while also nodding to Gieves & Hawkes' bespoke heritage. A collection that wholesales worldwide, Gieves may in turn entice men to step up to the next rung of personally tailored suits and, with more time and money, graduate to bespoke.

HOUSE STYLE

Of all the Savile Row tailors, it is fair to say that Gieves & Hawkes has avoided being pigeonholed into a particular style, silhouette or social status. Rock stars, royals, bankers and beatniks all benefit from Gieves & Hawkes' expertise as bespoke tailors. Literally anything is possible when bespoken by the customer.

PRESENT ROYAL WARRANTS

H.M. the Queen (livery & military tailors), H.R.H. the Duke of Edinburgh (naval tailors & outfitters), H.R.H. the Prince of Wales (tailors & outfitters).

FAMOUS/INFAMOUS CUSTOMERS

King George III, the Prince Regent (later King George IV), Admiral Lord Nelson, the Duke of Wellington, Captain Bligh (of *Mutiny on the Bounty* fame), Mr. Stanley & Dr. Livingstone, George V, Kaiser Wilhelm, Prince Abhakara of Siam, King Paul of the Hellenes, King Paul of Yugoslavia, King Michael of Romania, King Feisal of Iraq, Prince Juan of Spain, Emperor Haile Selassie, King Tupou of Tonga, the Kings of Denmark, Sweden and Norway, King Hussein and King Abdullah of Jordan, (former) King Constantine of Greece, Sultan Qaboos of Oman, the Sultan of Brunei, Roger Moore (as James Bond), Sir Bob Geldof, Edward Van Cutsem, Lord Freddie Windsor, the Princes William & Harry.

ADDRESS

GIEVES & HAWKES, 1 Savile Row, London W1S 3JR. Tel. +44 207 434 2001. www.gievesandhawkes.com

HENRY POOLE & CO.: THE GODFATHER OF SAVILE ROW

HISTORY

Henry Poole & Co. justifiably earned the title "Founder of Savile Row" when the eponymous proprietor made the Savile Row-side workshop of his father James's Old Burlington Street shop into a grand, Palladian entrance that stretched from no. 37 to no. 39 in 1846. Founded in 1806, James Poole and his wife Mary earned their reputation as military tailors to the officers' troops at the Battle of Waterloo. It was James who was invited by Queen Victoria to modernize court dress in 1869 from the frilly Georgian lace jabots and cuffs to a sleeker black velvet tailcoat, waistcoat and breeches in black silk velvet worn with a white wing collar and bow necktie. Despite the uniform reverting to Georgian style, court dress is still worn by High Sheriffs and still made by Henry Poole & Co.

Henry Poole is a legendary proprietor on Savile Row: a genius self-publicist for bespoke whose father recognized his garrulous side and financed him as the firm's ambassador to high society where Henry befriended (and dressed) Jem Mason (the winner of the first Grand National), the young Earl of Stafford (who scandalously married a circus rider) and Baron Meyer de Rothschild. In a calculated risk that belonged in a Baroness Orczy novel, Baron de Rothschild and Henry Poole advanced the man who would become Emperor Napoleon III £10,000 to stage a coup in France, earning Poole the first of its forty Royal Warrants in 1858.

At the accession of Emperor Napoleon and Eugenie, Henry Poole erected an audacious gas illuminated eagle-and-coronet light show above the façade of no. 36; a tradition the shop would repeat on all great royal occasions connected to Poole customers. A mere two years later, the 20-year-old Bertie, Prince of Wales (rakish son of Queen Victoria) placed his first order at Poole's. The Prince of Wales is traditionally the poster boy for Savile Row bespoke and Bertie's friendship with Henry Poole elevated the tailor into the top ranks of society in much the same way designers such as Gianni Versace and Tom Ford were later feted.

Poole's Savile Row address became the only building in London outside Marlborough House (Bertie's palace) where the Crown Prince of Prussia, the King of the Belgians, the Khedive of Egypt, Tsar Alexander II of Russia, King Umberto I of Italy and the doomed Emperor of Mexico held court alongside Prime Minister Disraeli, Lord Randolph Churchill, Lord Dupplin, Charles Dickens, Prince Bismarck and the Prince of Wales' mistress Lily Langtry.

It is this period of Poole's history from which one of the most controversial tailor's tales emerges. In 1860, the Prince of Wales ordered a short smoking jacket to wear at informal dinner parties at Sandringham: the first dinner jacket on record. In 1886 Mr. James Potter of Tuxedo Park, New York, was a houseguest at Sandringham. He consequently ordered a similar smoking jacket to the one worn by his host at Henry Poole & Co. It was this dinner jacket that Mr. Potter wore at the Tuxedo Park Club; inspiring numerous copies that members wore as informal uniform for stag dinners. Thus the tuxedo was born at Henry Poole & Co.

"Old Pooley" died in 1876 having penned a note declaring "there will be nothing much to leave behind me." The Savile Row tradition of extending credit to its aristocratic customers—and his undeniable taste for the high life—caught up with Henry Poole after he had extended unlimited credit to the Prince of Wales and his circle. The business had existed in much the same way as a St. James's Street gentleman's club like White's or The Athenaeum. The Ton (London society's leading men) would flock to no. 36 Savile Row between 3:30 p.m. and 5 p.m. to guzzle Pooley's hock, smoke his cigars and order bespoke suits by the dozen on credit.

The combined efforts of Henry's sister Mary Ann and his first cousin Samuel Cundey to retrench saved Henry Poole & Co. from extinction. Henry's estate was sold at Christie's in 1877 and the deathbed letter Henry wrote to Bertie was eventually answered with payment of the Prince's account and simultaneous withdrawal of his custom. By 1883, the grim reaper left 26-year-old Howard Cundey (Samuel's son) in charge and not a single Poole left.

"A fine specimen of a West End gentleman," Howard Cundey led the late Victorian crusade to end "sweated" labor on and around Savile Row, emerging as the definitive Edwardian bespoke proprietor. At once less garrulous and more professional than Henry, Poole under Howard Cundey gained a reputation (disputed later by Samuel) as the tailor who would not open his doors to a new customer unless he had two written introductions from reputable customers. As the *Daily Mail* sniped, "When William the Conqueror landed at Hastings the first use he made of his victory was to extort from the defeated nobles a letter of introduction to Poole's." Suffice to say, by the beginning of the twentieth century, Henry Poole was the largest establishment of its kind in the world, employing 300 tailors, 14 cutters and making 12,000 bespoke garments per year.

Bertie's return to Poole when he was crowned King Edward VII restored the Monarch's Royal Warrant to the shop: a chain that is unbroken to this day. American luminaries like William Randolph Hearst, Cornelius Vanderbilt and even Buffalo Bill (who, incidentally, dressed to the right) joined Far East potentates such as the Maharajah of Gaekwar of Baroda, the Maharajah of Cooch Behar and the Shah of Persia. It was in the Edwardian era that Howard opened Henry Poole & Co. embassies in Paris, Berlin and Vienna. In 1907, Howard Cundey acquired the few remaining shares of the company not in Cundey hands. Howard's son Hugh later justifiably remarked, "go through the pages of the *Almanack de Gotha* (the directory of European royal houses) from 1850 to the end of civilization in 1914 (when the storm clouds of WWI broke) and we could match page for page from the old ledgers."

Poole's head cutter, the monstrous German Mr. William Gustavus Brinkmann, was in place by 1897 and proceeded to terrorize both staff and customers until an altercation with the Duke of Marlborough forced the matter into court proceedings and dismissal. Poole's maintains that no war since Napoleonic times had ever benefited the firm despite its status as a noted military tailor. World War I toppled monarchies, irreversibly eroded the British aristocratic way of life (and dressing) and culled a generation of Europe's young men.

As a precursor to present chairman Angus Cundey's venture into Japan, Crown Prince Hirohito commissioned Henry Poole & Co. to create westernized suits for his state tour of Britain in 1921.

A representative of Poole's sailed for Gibraltar with pattern templates where he met the Crown Prince's destroyer and cabled measurements to London so the order would be accomplished three weeks later when the Prince reached the United Kingdom. Howard Cundey died in 1927 (swiftly followed by his wife) but not before giving his first and only interview with the press. The article was printed under the banner headline "Poole Has Spoken." The present chairman's father, Sam Cundey, inherited the business at the age of 22 along with double death duties. The business survived and Sam, with his brother Hugh, led Henry Poole & Co. into World War II in 1939.

A cable from Henry Poole's Paris branch captures the firm's spirit. "Much regret obliged to evacuate will communicate later (stop) Johnson." Like the infamous Windmill Theatre, where nude dancers performed "poses plastiques" while the bombs fell, Henry Poole kept its doors open on Savile Row for the duration of WWII. The business did suffer a dual direct hit when uncrowned King Edward VIII abolished frock coats at court and his successor George VI abolished court dress altogether in 1939 with the onset of WWII. General de Gaulle, leader of the free French in wartime London, became a customer, as did John Pierpont Jr. and Prime Minister Churchill. The post-war parity of pound and dollar made the fifties a rich seam of overseas trade for Henry Poole & Co., leading to journalist Lucius Beebe declaring "when you have a dinner jacket cut by Poole you are thus skirmishing with history."

March 1961 saw the tragic closure of Poole's grand Savile Row premises when the lease expired and the company was forced to relocate to 10-12 Cork Street. As *Henry Poole: Founders of Savile Row*, notes, "Sam Cundey's heart was broken." It was during this traumatic move that Sam's son Angus was instructed to sell three tons' weight of patterns for 18 pounds, 19 shillings and 9 pence for scrap. Gone were patterns cut for Napoleon III, Wilkie Collins, Charles Dickens and Edward VII. In 1974, at MD Angus Cundey's instigation, Henry Poole & Co. signed its first licensing deal with Matsuzakaya to stock ready-to-wear in the new wing of the Ginza. His father had licensed bespoke to Japan a decade earlier.

Angus Cundey assured the survival of Henry Poole & Co. through the swinging sixties and early seventies when Tommy Nutter dressed icons of the "youthquake" in his interpretation of bespoke. Like Nutter, Cundey banished frosted glass from the shop's windows and introduced window displays and press presentations of Savile Row bespoke to a new generation. In one of his last conversations with father Sam, Angus Cundey said he was "going to take the company back into the Row," and promptly did so in 1982.

No. 15 Savile Row was built in 1732 to the order of the third Earl of Burlington. Henrietta, Countess of Suffolk, retired as Lady-in-waiting to Queen Caroline (and mistress of her husband King George II) to live a dissolute life at no. 15 until her death in 1767. In 1871 the property became the Savile Club. The original house was demolished and rebuilt in 1887. It is in this property that Henry Poole & Co. operates from today. A new fifteen-year lease was signed in 2006, securing Henry Poole's future on Savile Row.

THE COMPANY TODAY

In 1986 Angus's son Simon Cundey trained at the London College of Fashion as a bespoke tailor and, after a secondment to Huddersfield textile mill Taylor & Lodge, joined the family firm. A trained cutter like his father, Simon Cundey is the firm's front-of-house man and oversees the company's regular annual visits to the USA, Europe, Middle East and Japan. The French connection the company forged with de Gaulle continues, with the firm dressing former President Giscard D'Estaing and Prime Minister Edouard Balladur. The company continues to dress the English aristocracy (Poole's is now on its fifth Duke of Bedford) and scions of the American banking dynasties. It currently holds the Royal Warrant of Queen Elizabeth II. Licensing agreements with China and Japan are in place, and chairman Angus Cundey remains firmly in the guv'nor's chair at no. 15 Savile Row.

HOUSE STYLE

As Angus Cundey delights in repeating, "Poole leads and others follow." It is the only firm on Savile Row that retains a tannoy system between the cutting room, stock rooms, workrooms and chairman's office, producing such pearls as "His Excellency has arrived, Mr. Cundey," or "I have the Royal Mews on the telephone." A set of jockey scales that Henry Poole installed in 1875 to keep a check on customers' weight between fittings is still on display, as are a royal flush of gilded Warrants and the sinister carved eagle insignia of Napoleon III. The shop is formal without being grand or overbearing and the cutting room (and increasingly the fitting rooms) are populated by bright young men. The company continues to innovate while never appearing vulgar or losing its sense of superiority as the Founder of Savile Row.

FAMOUS/INFAMOUS CUSTOMERS

H.I.M. the Emperor Napoleon III and Empress Eugenie, H.M. King Umberto I of Italy, H.G. the Duke of Aosta, H.R.H. the Prince of Wales (later King Edward VII), Lord Dupplin, Prime Minister Benjamin Disreali, Lord Cardigan (of the Light Brigade), J.P. Morgan, William Randolph Hearst, H.H. the Maharajah of Cooch Behar, H.I.M. the Shah of Persia, H.M. King George V, H.M. King George VI, H.I.M. Emperor Haile Selassie of Ethiopia, H.M. Queen Elizabeth II.

ADDRESS

HENRY POOLE & CO., 15 Savile Row, London W1S 3PJ. Tel. +44 207 734 5985. www.henrypoole.com

HUNTSMAN:
THE THOROUGHBREDS

HISTORY

Henry Huntsman founded his eponymous tailor's shop in 1849 specializing in breeches and sporting clothes. H. Huntsman & Sons was established on the Row at its present address in 1919. Like Anderson & Sheppard and Kilgour, French & Stanbury, Huntsman gained a reputation from the twenties onwards as a favorite of Hollywood screen idols.

Huntsman has benefited from very strong, charismatic leadership throughout the twentieth century. Brian Lishak, formerly of Huntsman and now a co-founder/director of Richard Anderson, recalls as a teenager assisting the then-ancient Mr. Robert Packer who took over the business from Henry Huntsman's two sons in 1932. As related in *The Savile Row Story*, Lishak recalls, "he had this talent—he loved clothes and he loved quality and he loved people and he put the whole thing together and the people adored him."

Under Packer, Huntsman pioneered complete in-house production for its bespoke suits without reliance on the usual army of outworkers who surround Savile Row. It may sound like a production line but, in fact, Huntsman were simply keeping their suits in the family and not allowing for anything other than immaculate, ingenious hands at every stage of the suit's construction. To demonstrate to the customer that Huntsman's philosophy was in no way mechanical, one of the two workshops was not connected to electricity at all.

Lishak, who made his first USA trip for Huntsman in the fifties when he was still a teenager, recalled epic sea voyages aboard the Queen Mary or the Queen Elizabeth during which various Savile Row houses would travel together before setting up shop in one of the New York hotels around Grand Central Station such as the Biltmore, the Roosevelt or the Murray Hill Hotel. Lishak recalled the incredulity of New York customs officers on discovering a box of stiff collars; similar, one would imagine, to a contemporary immigration official finding a suitcase-full of whalebone. "If a customer found Huntsman too expensive I'd direct him to Jones, Chalk & Dawson, J.C. Wells or Bobby Valentine," said Lishak.

1966 saw Huntsman honored to design suits for the victorious England team to wear when they competed in the World Cup (as a sad sign of the times, 2006 team captain David Beckham's choice of tailor for England was Armani). Brian Lishak was fortunate enough to have worked at Huntsman under Mr. Packer, and later MD Mr. Colin Hammick. Mr. Hammick was the kind of man who was sufficiently handsome and svelte to model Huntsman's neat, flared, one-button jacket, and yet reserved enough to cringe when he was voted one of Britain's best-dressed men. It was Hammick's ambition for Huntsman bespoke to "improve on the perfect fit" and by that he did not mean fitting the suit to the body, but enhancing the body with the Huntsman cut. As an 80-year-old Robert Packer replied when complimented for keeping his fine figure, "would you like me to take my jacket off, sir?"

Though in the eighties Huntsman insisted that there was the same amount of handiwork in a Huntsman suit as there was sixty-years ago, Italian designer ready-to-wear was still undercutting Savile Row bespoke significantly and craft was secondary to style in most men's opinions. In 1981 Huntsman had bowed to what they thought was the inevitable and began selling a ready-to-wear line produced by Chester Barrie. 1984 saw Huntsman ready-to-wear exported to

Barneys New York and Louis Boston. This began a decline in Huntsman's bespoke business that wasn't shored up until 2006. In 2002, a valiant (and intriguing) attempt by Huntsman to get hip included a bespoke service for designer Alexander McQueen (who briefly trained at Anderson & Sheppard under Mr. Hitchcock) made by Huntsman.

McQueen's bespoke collection added £1,000 to Huntsman's already peak prices for Savile Row. Though McQueen looked dandy posing in Huntsman's window alongside general manager Peter Smith for *L'Uomo Vogue*, the collaboration was short-lived. A couple of Gucci Group executives (who nominally owned McQueen's label) placed an order, and Elton John's partner David Furnish took delivery of a black frock coat embroidered with a jet bead peacock. After that the collaboration was quietly terminated.

THE COMPANY TODAY

In 2004 the venerable house flirted with liquidation but was saved by a gang of four sympathetic investors including present MD David Coleridge. In 2006 Tom Leonard reported in *The Daily Telegraph* that Huntsman's bespoke orders were up 37% from the previous year. It is Coleridge's ambition to "humanize the shop (and) attract younger staff and customers" and he told *The Telegraph* "I remember one of the Rothschilds coming in and saying 'My God! You've got women here!'" The house has gained momentum with the young scions of the Rothschild and Goldsmith families attending Huntsman's inaugural poker night in 2006. A best of British bespoke open day in 2006 that included bespoke shoemakers (Cleverley), hatters (Lock) and leather goods houses (Swaine Adeney Brigg) showed solidarity with Savile Row's brother companies on St. James's Street.

David Coleridge announced in 2006 that the perfection of a custom made Huntsman suit will retail for £2,000 (compared to a minimum £4,000 for bespoke). He hopes this custom made suit will be able to beat out top-end tailoring collections from Ralph Lauren, Tom Ford and Giorgio Armani's *Fatto A Mano Su Misura*.

HOUSE STYLE

Notoriously the most costly Savile Row tailor, the Huntsman

bespoke block is one of the most distinctive on the Row. The shoulders are sharp; the coat is slightly longer and more natural in appearance. The one-button cut is notoriously difficult to balance hence Huntsman's pride in it. The emphasis at Huntsman is on "a clean line, the cutting and construction methods producing clothing of considerable resilience and longevity. These qualities are achieved by hand tailoring at each stage of the garment's production." Huntsman has its in-house check rewoven in new color ways annually. The house was the first on the Row to develop a one-button cut in the fifties: a hybrid of a riding coat and a dinner jacket. Huntsman's 1PP cloth, woven in limited edition, is the highest grading wool receives: the tailoring equivalent of a D-Flawless diamond.

FAMOUS/INFAMOUS CUSTOMERS

H.M. Queen Victoria & Prince Albert, H.M. King Edward VII, H.R.H. the Prince of Wales (the Duke of Windsor), Gregory Peck, Lord Louis Mountbatten, King Umberto of Italy, King Alphonso of Spain, Katharine Hepburn, Humphrey Bogart, Ronald Reagan, Rex Harrison, Bing Crosby, Gregory Peck, Richard Mellon, Gianni Agnelli, Hubert de Givenchy, Sir Laurence Olivier, Vivien Leigh, Dirk Bogarde, Peter Ustinov, James Goldsmith (whose suits his son Zac still wears), Ronnie Woods and his son Tyrone, Stephen Fry.

ADDRESS

HUNTSMAN, 11 Savile Row, London W1S 3PS. Tel. +44 207 734 7441.
www.h-huntsman.com

The Page: Christian Mancini

WELSH & JEFFERIES:
THE OFFICER CLASS

HISTORY

In the grand tradition of bespoke tailors like Gieves, who established themselves in Plymouth close to the Admiralty, or Ede & Ravenscroft setting up shop close to the Inns of Court, Welsh & Jefferies opened in the early twentieth century on Eton High Street, where the firm specialized in making uniforms for England's most prestigious public school. Eton boys then, as now, wore a variation on white tie, top hat and tailcoat. Traditionally Eton educated the sons of the aristocracy, but by the Edwardian era the school embraced an influx of offspring from diverse social classes such as wealthy northern industrialists, American financial tycoons and Indian maharajahs. Welsh & Jefferies were thus perfectly placed to dress generations of significant men the in the new world order.

In 1917 (the year of the Russian Revolution), Welsh & Jeffries bought a property at the heart of fashionable St. James's at no. 15 Duke Street. Perhaps unbeknownst to Messrs. Welsh & Jefferies, owning the freehold of no. 15 assured the company's survival through two World Wars while other tailoring firms foundered. It was during the First

World War that Welsh & Jefferies built a reputation as a formidable military tailor. The firm made uniforms for the officers of many regiments, in particular the Rifle Brigade, the 60th Rifles (KRRC) and the Coldstream Guards. The house boasted that it had more generals in the British Army on its books than any other on Savile Row. Founder George Welsh lived until 1969 when the company was obliged to sell the precious Duke Street freehold and relocate to Savile Row in 1970. Post WWII, the boom time for military uniforms had ended and the company had to explore the civilian market. The continued success of the Eton shop meant that successive generations of international men of means had been introduced to bespoke tailoring by Welsh & Jefferies, so the company had laid the groundwork to make introductions into international markets. Even today, there are few countries in the world in which Welsh & Jefferies do not have a clientele.

The expansion of the company was due largely to MD Mr. Alan Cooper, who bought Welsh & Jefferies from the founders' surviving family members. "We're 100% old traditional—you might say old fashioned—with perhaps the military touch," said Cooper of a business that now encompassed business tycoons, officers of the Royal Greenjackets, Gurkhas, Coldstream Guards and, in 1990, H.R.H. the Prince of Wales, who confirmed Welsh & Jefferies' pedigree as a military tailor when he appointed the firm with his Royal Warrant as sole military tailor.

In 1994, Cooper was joined at Welsh & Jefferies by one of the finest cutters of his generation, Mr. Malcolm Plews. Plews had served for seventeen years at Gieves & Hawkes, worked for Norton & Sons during the John Granger era, and been head cutter at Dege before moving to Welsh & Jefferies. Cooper practically doubled his business in this era when he bought Leslie & Roberts, a venerable Old Burlington Street firm, from guv'nor Dennis O'Brien. In its heyday between the World Wars, Leslie & Roberts was one of the mightiest bespoke tailors in London, dressing everyone from silent movie star Valentino to Ribbentrop. Welsh & Jefferies absorbed Leslie & Roberts' impressive book filled with diplomats, aristocrats and the officer class.

In 2006, Alan Cooper retired and Malcolm Plews took the reins as managing director. The firm's name is still conducting business in Eton High Street as well as the present Savile Row shop.

THE COMPANY TODAY

Welsh & Jeffries is a small, neat shop with floor-to-ceiling glass windows through which you can see Plews demonstrating his craft at the cutting table. An entire wall is filled with works-in-progress and Plews is invariably interrupted on an hourly basis by customers old and new seeking reassurance from one of the most knowledgeable tailors today. The firm travels twice a year to the USA, as well as making regular trips to Zurich and Geneva for their big business clientele. One particular customer acquired through Leslie & Roberts still insists on his original tailor's labels being sewn into his Welsh & Jefferies suits.

Plews is well schooled and well liked. The late Harry Helman (the "Godfather of Savile Row") considered London College of Fashion-trained Plews his brightest *protégé*. He was photographed for *The Savile Row Story* toting Helman's silver-topped fox head cane and wearing Harry's Trilby at a rakish angle. The handover from Cooper to Plews has proved seamless, and the company's future at no. 20 Savile Row is assured for at least another decade.

HOUSE STYLE

If it is bespoken by the customer then Welsh & Jeffries can cut it. Anything is possible at this discreet and noble house.

ROYAL WARRANTS

H.R.H. the Prince of Wales (uniforms).

FAMOUS/INFAMOUS CUSTOMERS

Rudolph Valentino, Joachim von Ribbentrop, Prime Minister Sir Anthony Eden, Sir Winston Churchill.

ADDRESS

WELSH & JEFFRIES, 20 Savile Row, London W1S 3PR. Tel +44 207 734 3062.

THE NEW ESTABLISHMENT

SAVILE ROW W1
CITY OF WESTMINSTER

THE TAILORS
OZWALD BOATENG is seated atop the mailbox.
Flanking him are RICHARD JAMES and TIMOTHY EVEREST. Surrounding them
are models wearing the three tailors' creations.
Photographed by Michael Roberts on Savile Row, London, November 15, 1996.

Not so much tailors as designers who can actually stitch and sew,
Boateng, James, and Everest are a new breed of Savile Row clothier. Boateng
the youngest person ever to open his own
applies traditional bespoke techni

Bus 8476   HIGH FASHION.   HOUSE OF BOATENG   sundance
HIGHER DRAMA.   CHANNEL
THURSDAYS 9PM STARTING JUNE 22
1-800-OK-CABLE

OZWALD BOATENG:
THE BESPOKE COUTURIER

HISTORY

Forget comparing Ozwald Boateng to his Savile Row idol Tommy Nutter. Ozwald is a product of his times and has done as much to revitalize the Row as the late Mr. Nutter. His advent at the top of Savile Row (no. 9 Vigo Street) in 1993 injected some much-needed youth, energy, vigor and drive into the Row. As a colorist, Boateng brought exotic cloth and electric linings back to men's style after a dead decade of nineties ready-to-wear minimalism. As a self-publicist, Boateng has also brought the spotlight back to the Row as a mascot of the new establishment. In a March 1997 issue of *Vanity Fair* he posed for an iconic Michael Roberts photograph on Savile Row alongside Richard James and Timothy Everest in the magazine's "London Swings Again" issue.

Born in 1968 in London to Ghanaian parents, Ozwald Boateng has been a presence on the men's style scene from the age of 5, when his mother ordered his first bespoke suit: a purple two-piece not dissimilar to what is arguably his most iconic suit to date (on display in *The London Cut* exhibition at the Palazzo Pitti). Boateng cut a dash as a teenage Mod and staged his first runway show at the age of 23. By that point his style was set: long, lean bespoke suiting in a color palette similar to David Hockney.

Boateng defines his role on the Row as "rewriting established perceptions of Savile Row with a more contemporary twist on the classical form." His ambition was "to combine the essence of British heritage, global glamour and absolute luxury," and his mission is more than accomplished. Boateng unleashed his fashion-forward tailoring with a catwalk show in Paris for which he had little financing but immense faith and chutzpah. Needless to say, the show was the success that propelled him into no. 9 Vigo Street in 1993 and inaugurated his mission to "save Savile Row." As he told *The Independent* journalist Stuart Husband in 2006: "Let's cut to the chase. If we don't value it (the Row) enough, we're going to lose all that it represents. I've invested the most effort and money in talking-up this street. I've promoted it like crazy. Why? Because I think it's worth saving."

Boateng's bravado does cause his elders to raise their eyes to heaven and sigh, but there's no getting around the fact that his "loud and proud" approach to bespoke tailoring has done the Row a great service. As maverick Soho tailor Mark Powell, who Boateng modeled for in the eighties, told *The Independent*: "He is his own best advert for his own stuff. And he's always had this romantic notion of Savile Row. Sometimes he can get quite messianic about it."

As this book was being written, Boateng is pushing Savile Row to centralize production of bespoke garments and battling to save the English Heritage building on Savile Row from a scandalous demolition order. What for? For a tailoring academy or a boutique hotel with each room designed by a different Savile Row bespoke tailor. Boateng may be met with resistance but he is unstoppable. Even the company going bust briefly in 1998 didn't stop the Boateng Express. He pays attention to his bespoke business but is also a formidable presence in Milan, where he shows his own-label Bespoke Couture collection, and in Paris where he designed and presented the biannual menswear for the house of Givenchy for three years.

THE COMPANY TODAY

Boateng insists that his Bespoke business is booming. "We get footballers, film stars, heads of state, City boys and the odd gangster" as he told CNN. A show at the Victoria & Albert Museum marked his twentieth anniversary in the tailoring business. H.M. the Queen presented Boateng with an O.B.E. in recognition of his services to bespoke tailoring in 2006 and his portrait painted by Jonathan Yeo (at a particularly dark time in his life) now hangs in the bespoke room at no. 12A Savile Row. Boateng launched his first scent—Parfum Bespoke by Ozwald Boateng—in 2006 and new stand-alone stores are under discussion for London, Moscow and Dubai. Perhaps his greatest success in 2006 was the screening of *House of Boateng*, a documentary series directed and commissioned by Robert Redford for the Sundance Channel. Billboards and busses all over LA showed a tangerine-suited Ozwald Boateng under the caption "This Brit has designs on America" . . . and you'd better believe it.

HOUSE STYLE

Ozwald describes his cut as "crisp and structured with attention on flow and finish." The look is twenty-first century dandy in the true sense of the word: understated but extravagant and deeply personal.

FAMOUS/INFAMOUS CUSTOMERS

Daniel Day Lewis, Will Smith, Sir Anthony Hopkins, Usher, Delroy Lindo, Jason Statham, Jamie Foxx, Wesley Snipes, Nick Moran, Lennox Lewis, Westlife, Audley Harrison, Billy Zane, Lenny Kravitz, Paul Bettany, Mick Jagger, Lawrence Fishburne, Jude Law, Pierce Brosnan, Samuel L. Jackson, Sam (son of Richard) Branson, Joel Silver, Patrick Viera.

ADDRESS

OZWALD BOATENG BESPOKE, 12a Savile Row, London W1S 3PQ. Tel. +44 207 440 5230.
OZWALD BOATENG BESPOKE COUTURE (ready-to-wear), 9 Vigo Street, London W1X 1AL.
Tel. +44 207 437 0620. www.ozwaldboateng.co.uk

RICHARD ANDERSON:
A PERFECT PARTNERSHIP

HISTORY

Though the youngest bespoke tailoring house on the Row (opened in 2001), Richard Anderson is joined as co-founder and MD by the great Brian Lishak: a master tailor with fifty years' experience on Savile Row. Both Anderson and Lishak cut their teeth at the august house of Huntsman while they were still teenagers, but Lishak's career on the Row is a long and distinguished one.

At 16, he first experienced the Row in 1956 when it was still devastated by the Blitz, beginning his working life at H. Huntsman & Sons as a junior sales assistant in the accessory department and, subsequently, in the tailoring department. "I discovered another world of craft and skill, handed down from one generation to another with pride and love. I was enraptured and knew this was going to be my life," he recalls. "Soon I was to serve royalty, peers of the realm, kings of industry, people of note from all walks of life from countries all over the world. I still do today."

Lishak served his national service with the RAF between 1959 and 1961. He returned to Huntsman and was promoted to sales director in 1968. As the consummate front-of-house man, Lishak was soon sent on the traditional Savile Row tour of duty aboard the Queens Mary and Elizabeth steamships to the USA. He quickly earned a reputation for charming the glitterati on board and taking orders before the ship docked in New York. Lishak was surprised and delighted by the camaraderie of Savile Row abroad. "Here were all these competitors, all so friendly, it was extraordinary," he told *The Savile Row Story.* "There was absolutely no worry about looking after each other's customers—I went to Houston for Bobby Valentine and once when John Wells left all his orders behind, I brought them home for him. We'd even send customers to one another. If a customer found Huntsman too expensive I'd direct them to a colleague."

Lishak recalls visiting thirty-five cities per trip by train. At the time, Lishak says, "a lot of out customers were in awe of us. That's changed." Lishak was also an innovator who was the first on the Row to augment the tape measure with a camera to record his customers shape. As this golden period of Huntsman's history reached its sunset, Lishak left the firm and served eleven years between 1983 and 1994 at Wells of Mayfair before returning to his alma mater, where he became MD in 1997 and deputy chairman in 1999. It was during this time at Huntsman that Lishak met head cutter Richard Anderson. Like Lishak, Anderson had been working on Savile Row since his teens. In 1985 he had been sent on his first USA trip and began cutting for his own customers in 1987. He was the youngest head cutter in Huntsman's 150-year history.

As production director of Huntsman, Anderson was asked to create the cloth designs for the house's exclusive fabrics, including an annual reinterpretation of the Huntsman house check. Huntsman was eventually sold to outside investors and this decision prompted Lishak and Anderson to exit the house and launch Richard Anderson Ltd. at no. 13 Savile Row.

THE COMPANY TODAY

Since joining forces, Richard Anderson has made the house's name working with the finest cloths (Escorial, Guanashina, cotton/cashmere, stonewashed silk, Super 250's Worsted and Vicuna) while constantly innovating with bespoke suits featuring asymmetric pinstripe, cloth made from bamboo and cutting classics such as the dinner jacket in cloth encrusted with black sequins. Like many of the Savile Row bespoke houses, Richard Anderson also offers made-to-measure and a ready-to-wear collection.

Richard Anderson and Brian Lishak now take quarterly trips to the USA. In 2004, Richard Anderson acquired Strickland & Sons; a company that can trace its lineage back to 1780 and dressed Beau Brummell . . . as did all Savile Row firms in the early eighteenth century as the Beau exhausted his credit at one house after another. Strickland & Sons had a terrific customer base in Canada and the USA that proved useful for the fledgling company. Richard Anderson is a company keen to explore innovations in luxury cloth courtesy of Scabal, including a Super 150's Worsted woven with diamond chips and a cloth shot through with 22 karat gold.

No. 13 Savile Row is one of the most welcoming shop fronts on the Row. Jewel-bright cotton cashmere velvet jackets or an extraordinary pea coat cut from orange snooker table baize attract the eye in the open window. The mood and the décor is light, with cutting tables nonchalantly placed in the center of the store and fitting rooms in the rear. This is the kind of twenty-first century bespoke tailor that a man feels comfortable bringing his wife/girlfriend/boyfriend into for a fitting. Anderson and Lishak promote an open door policy that doesn't frighten prospective punters off with menacing moose's heads, snooty staff and club ties. The youngest bespoke firm on the Row is one of the street's strongest.

HOUSE STYLE

The Anderson line is "long and flattering, high cut on the armholes so the jacket doesn't ride-up." The shape is "slim and elegant," while the choice of cloth reflects Anderson's adventurous nature. Anderson continues to cut every bespoke suit himself.

FAMOUS/INFAMOUS CUSTOMERS

Sir Ian McKellen, Andre Leon Talley, Sebastian Horsley, Bryan Ferry, Westlife.

ADDRESS

RICHARD ANDERSON, Sherborne House, 13 Savile Row, London W1S 3PH. Tel. +44 207 734 0001. www.richardandersonltd.com

RICHARD JAMES
SAVILE ROW

RICHARD JAMES
SAVILE ROW

RICHARD JAMES
SAVILE ROW

RICHARD JAMES:
THE SHOWMAN

HISTORY

Richard James can quite rightly stake his claim as the first of the new
establishment bespoke tailors to open a shop on Savile Row in 1992.
Like his peers Ozwald Boateng, Nick Hart and Timothy Everest,
Welsh-born Richard James was attracted to London's fashion scene
and worked in one of the city's best finishing schools: Joan Burstein's
seminal South Molton Street boutique Browns.

Mrs. Burstein's windows have introduced John Galliano, Alexander
McQueen and Hussein Chalayan to London fashion. Her press office
unleashed Robert Forest (fashion's Rip Van With It) on the fashion
world and helped Richard James hone his vision of new generation
Savile Row menswear.

James and his business partner Sean Dixon were as alien to Savile
Row as Saturday opening hours and "fashion"; both of which James
promoted from the start. James offered bespoke suits not made on the
premises, placing the emphasis instead on made-to-measure and off-
the-peg that swiftly wholesaled to Bergdorf Goodman in New York
and Beams in Tokyo. His neighbors flung insults like "parasites," and

"at least they're not Boots the Chemist." Emotions were still relatively raw ten years later, when James posted these comments in his window to celebrate a decade on the Row. He is now a valued member of Savile Row Bespoke.

In 1997 the new Labor Party led by Tony Blair came to power. "Cool Britannia" kicked-in and found itself on the cover of *Vanity Fair*. Richard James dressed the notorious Gallagher brothers Noel and Liam for Oasis videos and wedding days alike. With a little help from Britpop and Blair, Richard James took off. But what he and Dixon did next is a lesson in survival for any bespoke tailor.

In 1995 Tom Ford initiated a very personal strategy to brand his own lifestyle and sell it under the Gucci label. The look—Studio 54 decadence, luxury and sex appeal—was applied to everything from cuff links to cafés in Milan. Richard James was Savile Row's answer to Tom Ford and put his name to a coherent collection of gentleman's requisites. Careful to work wherever possible with the best British factories, Richard James turned his attention to shirts, silk ties, biker leathers, Japanese loom-made low-rise jeans, t-shirts, Northampton-made dress shoes, cult Tretorn trainers, sunglasses, cuff links, luggage, cashmere, socks, underwear and his Savile Sport collection.

By August 2000, Richard James owned the largest shop space on Savile Row at no. 29. The "goldfish bowl" glass windows that slice Savile Row and Clifford Street at right angles are as breathtaking as an infinity pool. This transparency allows the neighbors a good view when "friends of the house" such as *GQ* Editor Dylan Jones, Elton John, Hugh Grant, Tom Cruise or Pete Doherty pop by for the bespoke service so many of his competitors insist he cannot provide.

THE COMPANY TODAY

In 2006 under the banner announcement "Richard James takes steps to secure the integrity of Savile Row," James and Dixon announced that they'd secured a second site from Pollen Estate landlords and would dedicate it to bespoke tailoring. The shop at 19 Clifford Street (opposite one face of the existing Richard James) will, according to James, "be more private. With all the windows our (existing) shop is a bit of a goldfish bowl and it becomes a bit of a spectacle when celebrities come in for fitting," he told a trade magazine with what must have been a Cheshire cat grin. No. 19 Clifford Street will be opened in Spring 2007. The previous season, James unveiled a new streamlined block that I called "Gym-toned tailoring" in the *Financial Times*. The block was released in an exclusive collaboration with Harvey Nichols.

HOUSE STYLE

James made an immediate impact on the Row with his color sense . . . including cutting two suits in camouflage fabric for Dustin Hoffman and Robert De Niro to wear on a famous 1998 cover of *George* magazine. James also was first off the mark with the long, lean one-button silhouette. He was the first to reinterpret a skinny black barathea dinner jacket made for a girl who happened to be in his shop when Pete Doherty came to call. Doherty tried it, liked it and commissioned the cut for his first bespoke suit that the rest of the world assumed was a Hedi Slimane for Dior Homme.

FAMOUS/INFAMOUS CUSTOMERS

Paul Bettany, Daniel Craig, David Beckham, Jude Law, Pete Doherty, Ralph Fiennes, Robbie Williams, Richard E. Grant, Tom Cruise, Bryan Ferry, Rio Ferdinand, Christian Lacroix, Craig McDean, Benicio Del Toro, David Linley, Elton John, David Furnish, the late Gianni Versace, Guy Ritchie, Jarvis Cocker, Manolo Blahnik, Mick Jagger, Michael Douglas, Nicole Kidman, H.R.H. the Duke of York, Nick Knight, Patrick Cox, Sir Paul McCartney, Hugh Grant, the Gallagher brothers, Madonna, Mario Testino.

ADDRESS

RICHARD JAMES, 29 Savile Row, London W1S 2EY. Tel. +44 207 434 0171. www.richardjames.co.uk

はい、それなりに気をつかっております

私のワードローブ

第五回 スペンサー・ハート／ディレクター **ニック・ハート**

サヴィルロウに新たに息を吹き込んだスペンサー・ハートのディレクター、ニック・ハートのワードローブを。
彼が手がけるスーツはシンプルながらも力強さを放っていた。
そこには彼のジェントルマンが目指すべきスタイルのヒントが隠されている。

Photography/Akemi Kurosaka
Text/Mari Miyama

ビジネスシーンでは黒のスーツ
"靴"を見せず"身体"を見せる

サヴィルロウのウインドウにディスプレイされているのはやはり黒。伝統はまだ
ベンダーには、で感じさせる古き良きイメージをまだ残していた。黒のスーツ
は一見、単に無難を通り越す何かを通り越すわけだ。1960年
代の伝統のスーツといったものに、甘ったるい感じがあるだけにシンプルなトリミ
ング。黒というカジュアルのスーツといったスタイルのうちの「カジュアル」という
力のトーンのシンプルスーツを着る。シンプルなところのバランス感覚を身につける
ハイデザインアップを目指すことだい感じが、そこにはハンガーのなか
ナイトのトーンから色のことトーンというのはそうしたのスーツのな
スーツという意味では、今黒いトーンとシンプルなデザイン。全体のトーンを基調に
し、強さがまだ黒で持ちなかったはじめに、完璧なデザインへと導く。

7 NICK HART

全身モノトーンだけど靴で遊ぶ

SU

トなスーツは黒にこだわる
これぞスペンサー・ハートといえるべき服身メタイ
ル。1つボタンが斬新的なトレンドに合色。クリエ
イティノな個性溢れの心の呼称を漂わすスーツ。

靴 で 遊

ニ

SPENCER HART:
THE SOUL BOY

HISTORY

Boy to man, Buckinghamshire-born Nick Hart has music in his soul.
Fortunately for Savile Row, he is as inspired by the style of his heroes
as he is about their music, be they jazz swingers (Louis Armstrong),
"old school" crooners (Frank Sinatra), Blue Note cool cats (Miles
Davis), Mambo Kings (Louis Prima) or the bebop idols and soul boys
of his youth.

It is this "rebirth of cool" nostalgic sensibility that Hart introduced
to Savile Row when, in 2002, he mortgaged his house to open
Spencer Hart: a bespoke, made-to-measure and off-the-peg business
named not after his son Spencer as so often reported but for his best
friend and "coolest guy I ever met" who tragically died.

Hart was no fool who rushed in where angels feared to tread. He had
successfully consulted for fashion brands like Joseph, Diesel, Voyage,
Mandarina Duck and Kenzo as well as new generation bespoke tailor
Timothy Everest. Hart approached the Row with a feeling that there
was a gap in the market as wide as Tony Blair's smile.

Hart admired the traditional bespoke houses like Poole, Huntsman and Gieves, who he continues to "watch with awe" as they execute uncompromising quality and craft. But his was a generation informed for most of the end of the twentieth century by the minimal, modernist clothing of Prada (designed by Neil Barrett), Jil Sander and Helmut Lang. He wanted to unite modern design and bespoke tailoring.

Taking an ostensibly simple but ineffably complex menswear manifesto, Spencer Hart set out to design and make "the perfect white shirt, the definitive black evening suit and so on." "Nick Hart taught me how to wear a suit," said Dan Peres, then editor-in-chief of USA men's glossy *Details*. "No matter which chic Italian label was sewn inside the suits I'd collected over the years I felt uncomfortable every time I put one on. In Spencer Hart suits I feel like myself and look a hell of a lot sharper." John Demsey, CEO of Estée Lauder and president of MAC Cosmetics, has four to six custom made Spencer Hart suits per season and calls the look "lots of style and a little bit of edge. He is one of London's leading resources for innovative style and design: the ultimate luxury brand for today's generation."

Robbie Williams remains Spencer Hart's most visible and vocal poster boy since the business hit the radar of the style press. A card declaring "Spencer Hart sincerely hopes you get laid in this product" cannot have failed to turn Robbie on to the clothes. Williams and the press attention he brought defied Savile Row's strict customer confidentiality clause (not that Hart cared much) and the Row called into question whether Spencer Hart was genuine bespoke or simply jazzed up made-to-measure.

Hart says that without style a suit can still be an ugly garment however whether it fits like a second skin or not. His mantra— "looking good is much more important than comfort"—could equally apply to the hairsplitting about what constitutes bespoke. If his clothes speak to a new generation then does it really matter if his suits aren't hand stitched for sixty hours by hobbits in a W1 basement?

Hart's fresh take on fifties formal suiting struck an unexpected cord with the hip hop fraternity who were an untapped market for Savile Row. After a boozy dinner at Les Trois Garçons in E1, Hart met and started dressing Damon Dash . . . the MTV generation's Ozymandias.

Dash dished to Kanye West and Jay-Z who paid Spencer Hart a visit. But Hart's reputation was sealed in his eyes when idol David Bowie, the Thin White Duke himself, became a client. "While sourcing clothes for David Bowie's world tour, I was completely bowled over with how beautiful the tailoring and fabrics were in every way," says Bowie's stylist Jimmy King. "David is a huge fan."

Who is left for Nick Hart to dress? "I'd do Beckham for free to get him out of those big tie knots and wide lapels," Hart told *The Independent* in 2006. "For me it's about Dennis Hopper, Steve McQueen, the guys at school who could dance and you always wanted to be with. I can make men look cool. That's the point." The sentiment sounds smug if you miss the spark in Nick Hart's eye as he says it. But it's the truth and nothing less than that which his competitors claim and don't deliver. Cool is a precious commodity, and Nick Hart has it.

THE HOUSE TODAY

No. 36 Savile Row gets better with age. The labyrinthine dark timber tunnel whose hand stitched leather floor leads visitors past spot-lit jackets towards the inner *sanctum* is still part cigar bar and part speakeasy, even though Nick has quit the Cubans. Jazz, soul and swing are still subtly piped into the shop and form the perfect soundtrack to Hart's melodic tailoring. Spencer Hart's bespoke and made-to-measure remix styles hark from the periods Nick admires, and a man comes out looking totally grounded in the twenty-first century. His glamorous assistants at no. 36, Petter and Anthony, emanate the same laidback, cool confidence proffered by big boss. A ready-to-wear "Nick Hart" label made its debut at the Paris collections in 2006 and is under development in Japan and the USA. In 2006 Aquascutum's CEO Kim Winser invited Nick Hart to reassess the British heritage brand's tailoring for autumn/winter 2006 with a sub-brand "Nick Hart for Aquascutum."

HOUSE STYLE

Despite setting up shop on the west side of Savile Row, Hart is not "one of the new school who make crap quality but pretend it isn't." Hart is adamant that his bespoke service (starting at £3,500) will live up to the benchmark set by traditional Savile Row while taking a totally contemporary approach to the silhouette. His style is unmistakable: white shirting lines his bespoke pieces, best described as skinny shawl collared or peak lapelled suits and frock coats in textured black, anthracite or midnight Moxon silk/wool blends and crisp white evening shirts with Marcella (dimpled) bibs and collars. Romantic details such as silk twill trims, complex hidden canvas pockets in his travel coats or whippet-thin silk ties are stars in the Spencer Hart universe.

FAMOUS/INFAMOUS CUSTOMERS

David Bowie, Robbie Williams, Duran Duran's John Taylor, Tommy Hilfiger, Matthew Williamson, Estée Lauder CEO John Demsey, Lawrence Dallaglio, Kanye West, Jay-Z, Jamie Foxx, Michael Roberts, Keane, Placebo

ADDRESS

SPENCER HART, 36 Savile Row, London W1S 3QB. Tel. +44 207 434 0000. www.spencerhart.com

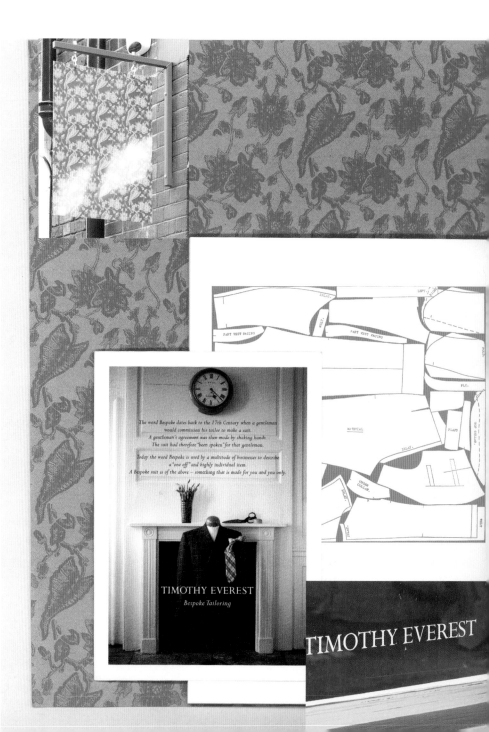

The word Bespoke dates back to the 17th Century when a gentleman
would commission his tailor to make a suit.
A gentleman's agreement was then made by shaking hands.
The suit had therefore "been spoken" for that gentleman.

Today the word Bespoke is used by a multitude of businesses to describe
a "one off" and highly individual item.
A Bespoke suit is of the above – something that is made for you and you only.

TIMOTHY EVEREST
Bespoke Tailoring

TIMOTHY EVEREST

TIMOTHY EVEREST: THE EASTENDER

HISTORY

To grasp Timothy Everest's unique perspective on bespoke tailoring you need three pieces of information. As a little boy he wanted to be a racing driver in the tradition of Glorious Goodwood, the London to Brighton rally and *Geneviève*. As a teenager growing up in Wales he began working for a large gentleman's outfitter called Hepworths that was to tailoring what the *Carry On* movies are to British film. Answering an advert "boy wanted for Savile Row tailor," Everest moved to London and into the world of genius manqué Tommy Nutter, where he worked on Savile Row alongside work placement student John Galliano who was perfecting his Mae West impersonation under the Nutter's watchful eye.

From these influences, possibly the most idiosyncratic of the new generation bespoke tailors was born. In 1991 Everest fell in love with a derelict house on Princelet Street in London's East End. Spitalfields has been home to generations of Huguenot and Jewish tailors since the sixteenth century. By 1991 it was the home territory of Britart with Gilbert & George and (later) Tracy

Emin as neighbors on the Georgian streets off Brick Lane. Opening a shop on Savile Row was comparable to "moving in with my parents" and Everest made a virtue out of his left field position in the cool East End that also happened to be much closer to the city than Savile Row. The business began as a ready-to-wear operation but bespoke naturally followed in this quarter resonant with the history of handcrafted clothing. In 1996 Everest unveiled his new Georgian townhouse-cum-atelier on Elder Street in the house once occupied by Bloomsbury artist Mark Gertler. Painter Richard Clark fitted out the townhouse with distressed leather sofas, old style radiators and wooden school benches. Later hardcore pornographic prints depicting as many varieties of oral sex as there are yoga positions were added. A leading pillar of the bespoke tailoring new establishment, Everest could be as traditional as Henry Poole or as subversive as Tommy Nutter depending on the customer's dictates. The Everest look was both British but modern and traditional but eccentric. 2000 began a three-year collaboration with Daks as creative director, during which Everest launched the E1 collection, heralding the heritage brand's attempted return to splendor. His collaboration with Marks & Spencer helped give the company's menswear a hip replacement. His consultancies have been as diverse as hip hop artist Damon Dash, Levi's, Kim Jones and Italian shoemaker Regain. These are the building blocks with which Tim Everest explored making his name a global brand.

THE COMPANY TODAY

Everest dipped his toe into Savile Row territory in 2005, opening a tailor's atelier on Bruton Place behind Stella McCartney and Matthew Williamson, and around the corner from Martin Margiela. He has developed a bespoke denim collection manufactured in Japan in September 2006, pioneering Savile Row tailoring patterns Prince of Wales check and dogtooth for limited edition bespoke jeans as well as unwashed blue and white cuts. The collection was launched at member's club Celux above the Louis Vuitton building in Tokyo's Omotesando district.

With his unerring radar for a city's erogenous zones, Everest opened a retail space in New York City's meat packing district in fall 2006.

The concept is owned by Bumble & Bumble CEO Michael Gordon, who thought Everest's cool bespoke tailoring was sympathetic to his own made-to-measure hairdressing empire. Gordon claims he found Everest after three out of four grooming editors on the London glossies were suited by him. Timothy Everest's USA ambitions do not end in Greenwich Village. He launched a ready-to-wear collection exclusively for Bloomingdales in San Francisco in September 2006.

HOUSE STYLE

Traditional patterns of dogtooth, Prince of Wales check and herringbone are cut into three-piece suits and town overcoats, but with details that set bespoke suiting apart from the rest. Pique trim, braiding, elbow patches, jetted pockets, sugar pink silk linings and deep purple under collars are all idiosyncrasies of Timothy Everest bespoke and he has adopted the Spitalfield flower (signature pattern of the Huguenot weavers and tailors) as an emblem on cuff links and jacket sleeves. You'll always find an echo of Tommy Nutter's early seventies heyday in Everest bespoke, though not sufficient to make it clownish or nostalgic.

FAMOUS/INFAMOUS CUSTOMERS

Tom Cruise, David Beckham, David Cameron, Gordon Brown, Kaiser Chiefs, Brad Pitt, Kevin Bacon and Mick Jagger.

ADDRESS

TIMOTHY EVEREST, 32 Elder Street, London E1 6BT. Tel. +44 207 377 5770. 35 Bruton Place, London W1J 6NS. Tel. + 44 207 629 5770. www.timothyeverest.co.uk

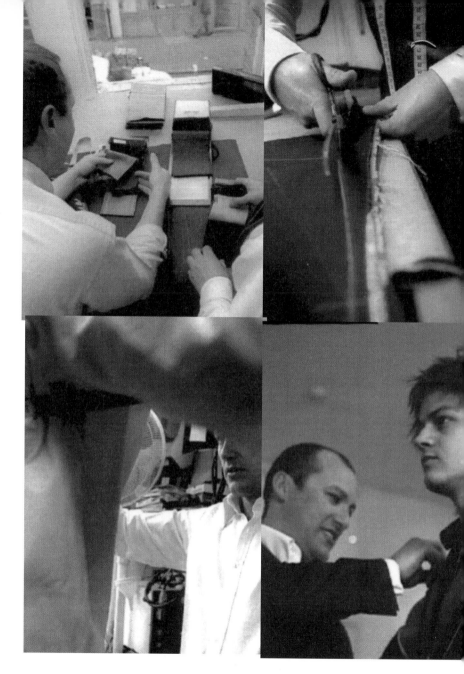

TONY LUTWYCHE:
THE BESPOKE ENTREPRENEUR

HISTORY

Lutwyche Bespoke founder Tony Lutwyche served in the $9^{th}/12^{th}$ Royal Lancers (Prince of Wales's) regiment for a decade. His Colonel-in-Chief was H.M. Queen Elizabeth the Queen Mother. Lutwyche rose to the rank of major and was posted to Germany, Northern Ireland and Bosnia before he decided that "ten years and all that excitement—crawling around with daggers in your teeth and so forth—was enough." In 1999 he left the British army and considered working in London. When asked at one of his many interviews with London firms how he would invest one million pounds, Lutwyche gave the answer his potential boss wished to hear (invest in the burgeoning Internet industry stock). "Actually, the voice inside my head said that if I had one million pounds I would rather like to open a bespoke tailoring business," he admits.

In 2000 Lutwyche exchanged the computer screen, mobile and BlackBerry of a Goldman Sachs city boy in favor of a cutting table, thimble and shears (wielded by a swiftly assembled team of experienced tailors) in a Soho townhouse colonized by fellow tailors.

Working from ground zero, Lutwyche built his book with young city gents he would visit in their offices on his moped, earning him the moniker "suiter on a scooter." He has since graduated to a Mini especially customized for him in pinstripe "due to an increasing number of client deliveries and the unpredictable British weather." Lutwyche Bespoke moved to the top floor of no. 83 Berwick Street when it outgrew the room he was subletting from a neighboring tailor. The building is a visceral example of Soho's great tradition as the home of bespoke tailoring workshops. As Lutwyche rather bluntly puts it, "if tailoring's heart is in Savile Row, then its guts are in Soho." Lutwyche had read the runes about Savile Row and his verdict was that "with the constant bullying from landlords on the Row, pushing existing businesses out by doubling their rates and halving their workspace, is it any wonder why people are starting to move elsewhere?"

Once you reach the fourth floor of no. 83, Lutwyche Bespoke is a slick, masculine clubroom with a fitting room, bespoke library and office. It is laidback and informal, perfectly complimenting Lutwyche's book of city boys, politicians, show business, sport and media men. "Men's fashion is evolving," he says. "My customers no longer want to buy off-the-peg. They come to me to receive premiere service and a unique, quality product that fits perfectly and reflects and flatters them as individuals."

THE COMPANY TODAY

Lutwyche Bespoke remains a discreet, by-appointment business and Tony Lutwyche is much less eager than his contemporaries to shout about celebrity customers. Only when a customer such as Paul Bettany tells the press he is wearing Lutwyche Bespoke (for the premier of *The Da Vinci Code*) does word get out. Lutwyche is adamant that he will see each of his bespoke customers personally and keep his finger on the pulse of the business. In 2006 Lutwyche and his investors bought the mighty Cheshire Clothing Company in Crewe. Renaming it Cheshire Bespoke, the new MD Tony Lutwyche is refocusing the business to produce made-to-measure and bespoke suiting for quality British brands that must remain nameless.

HOUSE STYLE
Disciplined, sharp and modern, Lutwyche Bespoke addresses the way men want to dress in the twenty-first century. Lutwyche is as comfortable creating immaculate morning dress as he is with a cornflower blue cashmere corduroy summer suit he made for a groom in Tuscany and subsequently for *The London Cut*.

FAMOUS/INFAMOUS CUSTOMERS
Hugh Dancy, Michael Sheen, Jamie Cullum, Gordon Ramsey, Tom Voyce, England's polo team, Paul Bettany.

ADDRESS
LUTWYCHE BESPOKE, 83 Berwick Street, Soho, London W1F 8TS. Tel. +44 207 292 0640. www.lutwyche.co.uk

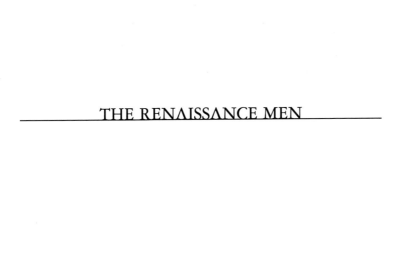

THE RENAISSANCE MEN

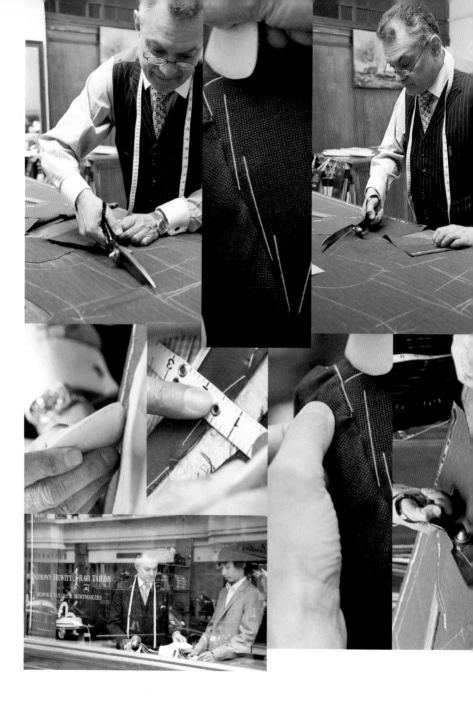

ANTHONY J. HEWITT:
THE CHAMELEON

HISTORY

In business since 1966 and on the Row since 1976, Anthony J. Hewitt's was a remarkable rise from a third floor room on Clifford Street to no. 9 Savile Row, where he incorporated Vincent's of Savile Row and Burlington Uniforms (a company that had developed a lucrative business making uniforms for industry). It was, however, written in the stars. Hewitt's auntie was a keen follower of the mystic Joseph Benjamin of Highgate and persuaded her 21-year-old nephew to attend a sitting with Mr. Benjamin. With no prompting from Hewitt, the mystic foretold that one day he would have a shop on Savile Row.

Whether it was a self-fulfilling prophecy or not, Hewitt became an apprentice coat maker at Gieves & Hawkes in 1951 and went on to apprentice as a trouser maker for Sanders of Savile Row. He graduated to train as a striker/trimmer at Anderson & Sheppard where he was inducted into the mysteries of the firm's famous "limp look." According to *The Savile Row Story*, Hewitt "discovered he had a natural flair" and became a cutter at Anderson & Sheppard.

Hewitt gained broad experience as head cutter at W. Prittard (a civilian and military tailor), head cutter for Austin Reed's bespoke department in 1963, and as an independent tailor first at 47 Carnaby Street in 1966 and then in Clifford Street in 1970. Spotting a gap in the bespoke trade for making quality uniforms for the hotel trade, Hewitt established Burlington uniforms in 1973 (a business now run by his son and MD Adrian Hewitt). The Row beckoned for the burgeoning companies in 1976.

In 1979 a young chap named Ravi Tailor joined Anthony J. Hewitt as a striker alongside cutter James Levett. Between them, Levett and Tailor developed Hewitt's business, with Levett bringing more of a Huntsman cut to the house and Tailor developing a hybrid style of his own invention. For most of the eighties Anthony J. Hewitt rode the boom in Middle Eastern oil money that gushed over Savile Row and developed a strong relationship with the USA. On one of his trips, Levett returned with a record 200 orders. Hewitt's panache as a maker of uniforms was tested when he was asked to design Guards-style uniforms for the Knights of Malta.

A.J. Hewitt has very discreetly "crossed the floor" to lend fashion designers such as Georgina Godley, Paul Smith, Koji Tatsuno and a young Richard James their expertise. Both Levett and Tailor were given these outside projects to execute, and in James's fledgling days Jim Levett would make Richard James's bespoke orders. He continued to do so after leaving A.J. Hewitt to set up shop under his own name further down the Row. Thus it was Ravi Tailor, not James Levett, who finally took the reigns from Anthony Hewitt when the founder retired in 2004, rechristening the firm Anthony J. Hewitt. Ravi Tailor's journey from Northern Rhodesia in the fifties to Savile Row is an epic tale. His father and grandfather before him had built up bespoke businesses in India attending to the officers and administrators of the British Raj before moving to Rhodesia (rechristened Zambia since independence was declared in 1964). A child of the twilight years of the Raj, Tailor attended boarding school at the age of 14, but President Kenneth Kaunda subsequently closed it when diamonds were discovered on school land. Tailor and his brother were drafted to replace his ailing father in the family's tailoring business.

Both inexperienced teenage boys learned on their feet from the
London Tailor & Cutter Manual. In 1973 Zambia's government
disintegrated and Tailor set sail for London where he trained at the
London College of Fashion by night while attending Perivale College
by day. In 1979 he joined Anthony J. Hewitt Ltd., remaining there
for the next twenty-seven years where he rose to become head cutter
and, eventually, managing director. In 1998, A.J. Hewitt acquired
the colonial bespoke tailoring specialist Airey & Wheeler, and in
2004 Anthony Hewitt took semi-retirement and Tailor became MD.
Founded in 1883 by James Airey and James Richard Wheeler, Airey
& Wheeler was a mighty presence on Regent Street, specializing in
lightweight and tropical ready-made clothing. Wheeler was the
showman and Airey the bespoke cutter for the house and their start
up capital was a mere £300. The present MD Anthony Airey's great-
grandfather became the sole trader upon Mr. Wheeler's death. Airey's
grandfather John inherited the business when his father's deathbed
will bypassed his brother James, who was a drunkard and a wastrel.
John Airey secured his family firm's future when he acquired the
freehold of 219 Oxford Street. This remained in the family until
1993. After the Second World War, John's sons joined Airey &
Wheeler. They became partners in 1947. Anthony Airey's father took
the adventurous step of introducing lightweight wool/Terylene suits
to the firm; an initiative Savile Row frowned upon. Shops in
Piccadilly and Sackville Street extended the Airey & Wheeler Empire
and turnover exceeded one million pounds until 1990. That year,
Iraq invaded Kuwait, effectively putting a stop to travel in the
Middle East, and by 1996 the company went into administration.
Anthony Airey and his wife Susan formed Vellair Clothing Company
in 1996 and bought the bespoke tailoring business from the
administrators along with the right to trade as Airey and Wheeler.
The business moved to no. 9 Savile Row in 1998 when it was
acquired by A.J. Hewitt, and Anthony Airey went with it. Airey and
Wheeler today are synonymous with the British man abroad; be he a
high commissioner, ambassador or business tycoon.

THE COMPANY TODAY
2006 marked the company's thirtieth anniversary year and Anthony

J. Hewitt negotiated a deal to share its shop front with the mighty Japanese denim company Evisu while retaining workshops and the listed oak-paneled fitting rooms. The co-habitation deal appears to be working and is reflected in the slightly more modest price tags for bespoke (from £1900). Lightweight and tropical suiting is a house specialty, and Mr. Tailor is developing a bespoke service for Evisu, which will in turn develop a collection of Airey & Wheeler ready-to-wear. Anthony J. Hewitt retains the rights to produce Airey & Wheeler bespoke and continues its strong shirt making trade while developing the lightweight trade but concentrating on natural fibers. With India, Japan and Africa in the company's DNA, Anthony J. Hewitt has a rightful claim to being the most internationally diverse company on the Row.

HOUSE STYLE

In Mr. Tailor's words: "A soft, natural shoulder line and a sharpened waist with a soft rolled lapel and clean front."

FAMOUS/INFAMOUS CUSTOMERS

GQ editor Dylan Jones is a new convert to Anthony J. Hewitt. The house does not comment on its other bespoke customers, but Airey & Wheeler has dressed two Archbishops of Canterbury, not to mention H.R.H. the Duke of York, H.R.H. the Earl of Wessex, H.R.H. the Duke of Kent, the Rt. Hon. John Major, the Rt. Hon. Lord Weatherill, the Rt. Hon. Lord Howe, the Rt. Hon. Lord Owen, the Earl Ferrers, Sir Michael Angus, Sir Paul Girolami, Sir Roger Gibbs, Sir Angus Stirling and Martin Bell.

ADDRESS

ANTHONY J. HEWITT, 9 Savile Row, London W1S 3PF. Tel. +44 207 734 1505. www.aj-hewitt.co.uk

CHITTLEBOROUGH & MORGAN:
THE DOUBLE ACT

HISTORY

In the late sixties and early seventies, Savile Row was revolutionized by the advent of Tommy Nutter and Edward Sexton, who opened Nutters of Savile Row in 1969. The Nutter silhouette attracted a heady cocktail of swinging aristocrats and rock 'n' roll royalty. Having both been trained at firms that are bespoke tailoring aristocracy such as Kilgour, French & Stanbury and Davies & Son, Roy Chittleborough and Joseph Morgan were invited to join Nutters of Savile Row by the garrulous Mr. Nutter and his head cutter/co-founder Sexton.

The full story of the rise and fall of Nutters of Savile Row is told in the later chapter on Edward Sexton. Suffice it to say that Chittleborough and Morgan observed the *louche* early seventies heyday of Savile Row and rose above any personal differences that developed between the founders of the company. As Morgan says, "We were just interested in making beautiful clothes and all of the drama surrounding Tom and Edward tends to obscure the fact that every suit we made in those days was of the highest standard. We were all perfectionists."

"They were very good days for us," says Chittleborough, "and it was a lot of fun. But the work we produced was very serious. We weren't just messing about." Not that there weren't almost daily occurrences when a peer of the realm's trousers would be savaged by Sexton's bulldog and anyone from a page three girl (a topless model) to Twiggy could be found behind the changing room curtain. Chittleborough recalls being sent for a fitting to the country house of one of Tommy's friends only to find the interior designer in bed with two other men. "You couldn't make it up," says Chittleborough.

All of the cutters at Nutters became experts in the deceptively languid style Tommy Nutter favored. Aesthetically, Nutter suits were bravura displays of complex checks, tweeds, horizontal pinstripes and velvets all inter-cut into show stopping suits trimmed with *grosgrain*, silken cord or satin. Technically, they were a complex execution of bespoke tailoring at its best. Without the technique, Nutter would have been no more memorable than a Carnaby Street boutique designer. Without Tommy's flair, the house may not have ignited Savile Row the way that it unquestionably did. While Morgan and Sexton were on one of their regular forays to the USA in 1976 (taking orders of up to one hundred suits per trip), Nutter abruptly quit the business. He and Sexton couldn't find a compromise on how to move the business forward. So the man with his name above the door left it there while Sexton, Chittleborough and Morgan remained. By 1981, Sexton split from Chittleborough & Morgan. The glamorous clientele fragmented further: some had remained faithful to Tommy Nutter, who worked his way through Kilgour, French & Stanbury and Austin Reed before opening again in his own shop on Savile Row. Nutter passed away prematurely in 1994.

Chittleborough & Morgan endured as "survivors of the original Nutters" and continued to create simply beautiful bespoke clothing on Savile Row in the eighties while Sexton and Nutter explored ready-to-wear, international marketing and the high life. Rent wrangles forced Chittleborough & Morgan to seek a residency with the venerable Hogg, Sons & J.B. Johnstone in 1995: the only bespoke tailor to be controlled by lady guv'nor Dorothy Donaldson-Hudson

who was a suitably lacquered presence on the Row during the
Dynasty decade with her couture suits, estate jewelry and white
poodle Groovy in tow.

During Chittleborough & Morgan's residence, J.B. Johnstone's
octogenarian cutter Malcolm Johnstone still worked in the Clifford
Street shop, serving the last gasp of the British Empire (governor
generals and old colonials) while Donaldson-Hudson ruled the firm
that also incorporated Tautz & Co. Chittleborough & Morgan later
shared space at Maurice Sedwell under MD Andrew Ramroop in
1999. Having considered going in with Huntsman, the chaps
decided that they'd worked long and hard enough to give up their
names in exchange for space and Huntsman MD David Coleridge
suggested they consider setting up shop in the basement below no.
12 Savile Row. As of January 2006, Chittleborough & Morgan are
back on Savile Row.

THE HOUSE TODAY

Chittleborough & Morgan now do business from the basement of no.
12 Savile Row in a sparse, bright space dominated by two cutting
tables for the partners. The interior of Chittleborough & Morgan is
neither nostalgic nor fashionable. The stripped down, no-nonsense
décor and workshops clearly visible at the back of the space are all
totally in tune with a modern customer who is interested solely in a
perfectly crafted suit made by masters in their art. There are no
distractions from the man, his tailor, the suit and the mirror . . . not
even chairs.

The mood at Chittleborough & Morgan is brisk and efficient. The
company dresses the survivors of the Nutter era, their children,
their grandchildren and a fistful of renegade aristocrats and men in
the music industry. To their credit, Chittleborough & Morgan
have been quietly and carefully encouraging new blood on the
Row. They invited fledgling bespoke shoemakers Tony Gaziano
and Dean Girling to unveil the prototypes of Gaziano & Girling
bespoke and made-to-measure shoes to fellow tailors and
customers. Morgan is supportive of a talented young bespoke tailor
named Jsen Wintle who is destined for great things and already
has a firm foothold in Russia.

HOUSE STYLE

Whereas Nutter took lapels wide, shoulders high, coats tight on the hip and trousers to a voluminous extreme, Roy Chittleborough and Joseph Morgan cut a whippet-thin suit with high, tight armholes and roped shoulders with an almost hourglass cut on the waist that moulds the body into perfect posture.

FAMOUS/INFAMOUS CUSTOMERS

Brian Epstein, Charlie Watts, Mick Jagger, Elton John, Sir Paul McCartney, Jean-Charles de Castelbajac.

ADDRESS

CHITTLEBOROUGH & MORGAN, 12 Savile Row, London W1S 3PP. Tel. +44 207 437 6850.

HARDY AMIES:
COUTURE FOR MEN

HISTORY

In 1945 no. 14 Savile Row was a derelict husk of a Regency house that had suffered a direct hit during the Blitz. In happier times, it had been the townhouse of playwright and wit Richard Brinsley Sheridan. A loggia box overlooking the grand staircase was allegedly the place where Sheridan would perch and snipe at the passing trade below. Hardy Amies, who served in the British Intelligence service during the war, broke into no. 14 during a walk down the Row and decided to restore the building and open it as the first postwar haute couture house in London.

1946 was an interesting year in fashion. Paris was still on its knees, having been occupied by the Nazis. Most couturiers had closed their doors during the occupation. Coco Chanel, who allegedly collaborated, had not. But she was forced into exile after the liberation of Paris and thus the city lost its fashion leader. Another one would emerge in 1947 when Christian Dior launched the new look and put Paris back on the map. Actually it was a relatively old look based on the Belle Époque silhouette, but no matter, it dominated fashion for the next decade.

Hardy Amies had opened his doors the previous year. In London clothing was still rationed until well into the fifties, but the Dior effect had opened the door for a return to extravagant, nostalgic haute couture. He and fellow London couturier Norman Hartnell (whose atelier survives relatively untouched on Bruton Street, even though the label is currently dormant) became rather like the Hollywood gossip rivals Louella Parsons and Hedda Hopper: eternally locked in a rivalry that did neither of their reputations any harm.

Hartnell was already well established as the couturier who had created the celebrated Winterhalter-style white wardrobe for Queen Elizabeth (the Queen Mother) to wear in Paris in the thirties. He also dressed the Queen's daughters the Princesses Elizabeth and Margaret Rose. Hardy Amies first dressed Princess Elizabeth in 1952 and continued to do so when she became Queen in 1953. Queen Elizabeth II ushered in a golden age for London haute couture and Hardy Amies was awarded the Royal Warrant in 1955. Amies became a court dressmaker to the Queen and remained so until his retirement in 2002.

Though the house was inextricably associated with the Queen, it was anything but resistant to dynamic expansion on an international scale not dissimilar to his Parisian contemporary Pierre Cardin. The name was first licensed in 1958 (the Hardy Amies tie) when Sir Hardy launched a trio of scents called "Amie," "Fun," and the more prosaic "Hardy Amies for Men." By 1966 Amies had a licensing network as extensive as the old British Empire that reached as far as Canada, America, Australia, New Zealand and Japan. He'd already launched own-label knitwear, leather goods, eyewear and house wares in 1960, as well as a ready-to-wear men's collection in 1961. Just as Cardin and Paco Rabanne dressed seminal sixties futurist movies, so too did Amies, designing the suits for Stanley Kubrick's *2001: A Space Odyssey* in 1968.

Amies was a great character and a great sybarite. In later life he ordered vast quantities of bespoke suits from Norton & Sons. Norton's present MD Patrick Grant has Sir Hardy's accounts from the seventies that record his ordering up to forty suits in one visit alone. He became the authority on correct dress for English gentlemen. In 1981 he wrote his second autobiography *Still Here*

(lest we forgot) and followed it with *The Englishman's Suit* in 1994.
Rapid expansion in so many different directions inevitably led to a
loss of autonomy and, to a certain extent, control. The house's official
history records that the company had to repurchase Hardy Amies
from (chain store) Debenhams in 1980. By 1992 worldwide licensing
sales peaked in excess of £200 million from over forty licensees. So
much activity so far from no. 14 Savile Row made plenty of people
plenty of money. Meanwhile Amies, his lieutenants Ken Fleetwood
and Jon Moore and his *protégé* Ian Garlant continued to present
couture shows in the atelier to an elite clique of aristocratic ladies
such as Raine, Countess Spencer and Deborah, Duchess of
Devonshire. Amies was knighted by the Queen in 1996 and,
according to Garlant, became the self-appointed grand old man of
British fashion.

THE COMPANY TODAY

Sir Hardy's successor, creative director Ian Garlant, has been with the
house, boy to man. He is keen to preserve Hardy Amies' status as the
last great British couture house left in business (Hartnell having
closed in 1988). Garlant takes up the story. "From the outset Hardy
and I got on, though at first I was terrified of him. At first employed
as a general studio assistant, I was soon made his personal assistant. It
was an exhilarating and educational experience. I also found it deeply
reassuring to have found a place in the world that simultaneously
challenged and encouraged me. One evening at dinner Hardy's foot
lay close to mine. On enquiring as to the size of his feet he replied
'I've no idea.' It transpired all his shoes were tailor made. At his
request I tried on a shoe. It fitted perfectly. 'I think they'll fit. I have
a feeling you'll step into my shoes—in fact I'll leave them to you.'
They did, he did and I did."

The handover was not as smooth as this rather glib story relates. In
fact it was positively Shakespearean. Long before Sir Hardy's official
retirement, the couture collection and clothes by appointment to the
Queen had been designed by Jon Moore, who was very much a
discreet presence in the atelier. Kenneth Fleetwood (the love of Sir
Hardy's life) was his anointed successor, while a young Garlant's
domain was the gentleman's bespoke salon on the ground floor of no.

14 Savile Row. Fleetwood's unexpected death upset the balance of power in the house and while Sir Hardy became the grandest of grand old men, Hardy Amies as a going concern lost its foothold in the here and now amidst infighting and not a little bitterness.

Sir Hardy's death in 2003 was followed by a new regime called the Luxury Brands Group, which also acquired the extinct House of Hartnell. Wishing to imitate Burberry's phenomenal re-branding as a British heritage/Cool Britannia brand operating on a global scale, the Luxury Brands Group almost toppled the house of Hardy Amies. Garlant had gone to consider the re-branding of another company wishing to do a Burberry called Aquascutum. Jacques Azagury, a favorite designer of the late Diana Princess of Wales, even stepped in briefly to create the couture collection, but did not settle at the house.

Before long Ian Garlant returned as creative director with Tim Maltin as inspiring MD. In 2003, the year of Sir Hardy's death, the company opened its first standalone store outside of no. 14 Savile Row in Ginza, Tokyo. In April 2006 Hardy Amies celebrated its sixtieth anniversary with a fashion show at the Victoria & Albert Museum. The house re-launched a licensed menswear collection designed from no. 14 in autumn/winter 2006. Biannual couture collections are designed by Garlant and shown at the house as Sir Hardy Amies would have wished it.

HOUSE STYLE

One of Garlant's (and Sir Hardy's) signatures is the Ghillie collar and the Stand collar on an elongated coat. Garlant favors an extravagantly waisted suit jacket and the frock coat for town but, as he says, whatever the customer bespeaks can be done.

FAMOUS/INFAMOUS CUSTOMERS

H.M. the Queen, Ava Gardner, Deborah Kerr, Deborah, Dowager Duchess of Devonshire, Raine, Countess Spencer, Jenson Button, the Osbourne Family, Freddie Ljungberg and Jacobi Anstruther-Gough-Calthorpe.

ADDRESS

HARDY AMIES, 14 Savile Row, London W1S 3NJ. Tel. +44 207 734 2436. www.hardyamies.com

Kilgour
Savile Row

KILGOUR:
EXTREME MAKEOVER

HISTORY

Along with Poole, Gieves, Huntsman and Anderson & Sheppard,
Kilgour, French & Stanbury is one of the foundation stone firms of
old Savile Row. Kilgour, as staff and customers alike always knew it,
may trace its roots back to 1882, but the company really came alive
during the jazz era. In 1923 two well-respected tailors, A.H. Kilgour
and T.F. French, united to form Kilgour & French. The Stanbury
brothers Fred and Louis, Hungarian immigrants, arrived in 1925 and
have since gone down in the annals of Savile Row history and
eclipsed Mr. Kilgour and Mr. French. In honor of their contribution
to the firm's fortunes, the house was renamed Kilgour, French &
Stanbury in 1937.

The company's archives were completely destroyed by fire in 1982
erasing almost all of the firm's early history but for a document
signed by Mr. Kilgour and a twenties graphic logo that the present
creative director, Carlo Brandelli, has since revived. The most
precious piece of the company's archive is a book containing Fred
Stanbury's sketches (a rarity on the Row) and an anecdote about Louis

Stanbury. If Fred became a well-liked patriarch of Savile Row, Louis is remembered as a tailor not dissimilar to Mr. Scholte: domineering, ostentatious and a great character.

"Fred was the technician and Louis was the showman," recalls Alan Bennett, MD of Davies & Son. "When you went into Kilgour you didn't go wearing your old tailor's clothes. You put on your best suit. I remember going in to see Louis wearing a suit I'd recently made for myself. Louis looked me up and down and said, 'That's a nice bit of work.' Then he took his chalk and marked a buttonhole on my lapel. 'When you go back to work, better put a buttonhole on that. It'll look grand.' Louis was really the salesman. He was the front-of-house man while Fred was the cutter."

Old timers like one of the street's most talented cutters remember Fred Stanbury, who predeceased Louis, today. 16-year-old Edward Sexton was an apprentice to Mr. Stanbury and recalls him being a formidable "master." Roy Chittleborough, MD of Chittleborough & Morgan, also trained at the firm. As Kilgour quite rightly declares, "the apprenticeship at Kilgour is still coveted by every young tailor, and the list of graduates of the firm's workshops reads like a modern day Savile Row roll call."

One gets the impression that Kilgour was "fast" as they said in the twenties when describing a risqué, frisky person. The company was sufficiently sophisticated not to turn away actors such as Fred Astaire, who had his iconic tailcoats cut at Kilgour and Anderson & Sheppard. Astaire wore white tie and tails with the same casual air as we wear jeans today and it was Kilgour's cut that the dancing man was wearing in his iconic 1934 film *Top Hat*. The film stills circled the globe and are still held up today as the epitome of male elegance. Kilgour was firmly on the map as the bespoke tailor to Hollywood royalty, and even Louis B. Meyer himself—the big boss at MGM (the film company that boasted more stars than there are in heaven)—chose Kilgour, French & Stanbury to clothe his fat frame. Power players such as Joseph Kennedy, father of JFK, lover of Gloria Swanson and USA ambassador to the Court of St. James's; the fabulously wealthy and glamorous Maharaja of Jaipur and Aga Khan (husband of Rita Hayworth) were all customers of Kilgour.

The most highly prized of Kilgour's VIP customers is Cary Grant.

Affable, elegant, sexy Cary Grant wore Kilgour suits both on and off the silver screen. His blue two-piece worn in Hitchcock's *North by Northwest* (1959) is as famous as Audrey Hepburn's little black Givenchy dress in *Breakfast at Tiffany's* (1961). Grant's character wore it throughout the movie as he is abducted, chased by a crop-spraying airplane and left dangling from Mount Rushmore. As *A History of Men's Fashion* declared of Grant: "The elegance of Cary Grant was of unruffled sobriety—a sign of serene Anglo-American distinction, his shoulders were more heavily padded than usual to make his head appear smaller, his suits were always impeccably cut, his ties understated. Cary Grant represented everything that was balanced in men's fashion. His tailor was Kilgour, French & Stanbury."

Grant was Kilgour's best advertisement for the lion's share of the sixties. Less well known was the fact that Frank Sinatra—who took great pride in his Italian roots and suits—was a Kilgour customer. Brandelli only discovered the Sinatra connection when he struck up a conversation with 74-year-old shirt maker Micky Smith. The story is told by Tim Blanks in *ES Magazine*. "Micky (said Brandelli), you must have seen some fantastic people." "Oh, yeah" said Micky pulling on a cigarette. "Well there was that American fella, used to do a bit of singing and acting . . . Frank something . . ." "Sinatra?" "Yeah, he was round the corner at the theater." "The London Palladium?" "Yeah, he was there with that friend of his; brought him in as well . . ." "Dean Martin?" "Yeah, that's the fella."

Kilgour welcomed the men and the moment. In 1968 the firm negotiated a license with Barneys, New York for a ready-to-wear collection, and in 1969 the firm pioneered research into manmade fabrics. To traditional minds, using manmades to create bespoke suits was like gilding a Rococo stateroom with crayons. The collection Kilgour developed is now in the Victoria & Albert Museum's textile collection. When Tommy Nutter and Edward Sexton parted company in 1974, Kilgour offered Nutter a place in the house. Though this must have been a sobering thought for the man who was briefly king of swinging Savile Row, the decision to hire Nutter shines a very kindly light on Fred Stanbury. The 1977 party to mark the opening of the refurbished shop at 33 Dover Street has become something of a legend. Soccer player George Best (who modeled the ready-to-wear collection) was among the guests. It also marked the last hurrah of the Stanbury brothers at Kilgour.

In one of those mergers and acquisitions that makes up the Row's history, in the early seventies Kilgour, French & Stanbury incorporated famed hunt specialist Bernard Weatherill who held the Royal Warrant of appointment to the Queen (riding clothes and uniforms), Queen Elizabeth the Queen Mother and the Duke of Edinburgh (livery tailors). Weatherill still retains its independence from Kilgour, and is the last maker of bespoke breeches in Britain. Though Kilgour, French & Stanbury retained the services of great craftsmen throughout the eighties and nineties such as Tom Leggatt (*The Savile Row Story* calls him "probably the most celebrated of modern perfectionists"), the *raison d'être* during this period was to ensure Kilgour employed the very best tailors and cutters. It was ruthless in pursuit of this goal, breaking ranks with its peers and paying above the market rates to secure the best work. Inevitably this created bad blood between the company and its neighbors, but Kilgour generated substantial licensing revenues in the Far East which were dependent on the firm's reputation as one of the great Savile Row bespoke tailors. All the while the glamour gradually faded, until present MD Hugh Holland hired a young Italian named Carlo Brandelli to reassess the company's past and future.

THE COMPANY TODAY

In 1998 Carlo Brandelli was asked to consult on the potential for Kilgour, French & Stanbury to reposition itself. One of Brandelli's first conditions was that the firm drop French and Stanbury in favor of the pithier brand name Kilgour (to rhyme with cigar). As creative director of Kilgour in 2003 after a management buyout, Brandelli sharpened the look of the shop and the "house style" tailoring block in a maneuver not dissimilar to Tom Ford's tenure at Gucci. Photographers Nick Knight and Sean Ellis were commissioned to shoot clean, contemporary images for the house, including a clever homage to David Hockney's *A Bigger Splash*.

Brandelli championed the single-button that elegantly elongates the frame and lengthens the torso. The first issue of *Men's Vogue* waxed lyrical about Kilgour's "lean, structured shoulders and the subtle uplift of the chest" quoting Brandelli as saying "if you don't have an athletic figure we'll give you one."

Brandelli's extreme makeover of Kilgour was radical but has been executed with the stealth of an assassin. Spots and stripes are his only permissible patterns and he's developed a unique navy Donegal cloth flecked with white baste stitch dots. Brandelli is an understated extremist and messianic about men's tailoring. Like his core customers, Brandelli is just under 40 years old: a time one wants to dress responsibly and stylishly rather than with the indiscriminate exuberance of a teenager. Like his fan base, Brandelli is also married with children. He's not a toxic bachelor.

The designer has "done" the London fashion scene. His father ran fashionable London restaurant L'Écu de France, where baby Brandelli was petted by the likes of Joan Collins. Fast-forward to 1993 and Carlo Brandelli opened directional menswear store Squire on the same site as Mr. Fish's old boutique on Clifford Street. The store dressed Britart and Britpop in its prime and then closed its doors. Brandelli came to Kilgour with that experience and the ruthless belief that "to design is to decide." Calling Savile Row "worse than draconian," Brandelli (with blessing of MD Hugh Holland) has kept the rest of the Row at arm's length. It's an echo of old Anderson & Sheppard's attitude to its peers.

Like Boateng, Everest and James, Kilgour's ambition is to be the first global luxury brand to emerge from Savile Row. His challenge is to take bespoke tailoring's "fanaticism to the point of fetishism" and apply this perfection to made-to-measure and ready-to-wear. In 2005 *GQ* named Brandelli Most Stylish Man of the Year and the British Fashion Council awarded him Menswear Designer of the Year. *GQ*'s interest and Jaguar's gifting of a new XK coupé model to the designer is a strong indication that "brand Brandelli" is working for Kilgour. Chaumet, Apple, Adidas and Ruinart champagne are stealthily enhanced by Brandelli's endorsement.

HOUSE STYLE

The one-button single-breasted suit in seasonal cloth worn with a classic white shirt and knitted tie or scarf. Brandelli's particular trademark is the polka dot woven into the cloth. He describes the Kilgour line as "long, elegant and athletic with a neat, structured shoulder."

FAMOUS/INFAMOUS CUSTOMERS

Fred Astaire, Louis B. Meyer, Sir Francis Chichester, Joseph Kennedy, Edward G. Robinson, Cary Grant, Ava Gardner, Jackie Kennedy, Charles Laughton, Rex Harrison, Robert Mitchum, Adnan Khashoggi, King Faisal of Egypt, Crown Prince Akihito of Japan, the Duke of Bedford, H.H. Prince Amyn Aga Khan, Sir Harold Pinter, Frankie Vaughan, Lord Forte, George Best, Jude Law, Hugh Grant, Noel Gallagher, Bryan Ferry, Peter Saville, Thomas Lenthal, DJ Pete Tong, Pet Shop Boy Chris Lowe, Eric Clapton, David Gray, David Lean, Mantovani, Tim Roth, Primal Scream's Bobby Gillespie, Rankin, Sean Ellis, Roland Mouret, Michael Owen, Jamie Redknapp, Little Britain comedian David Williams, David LaChapelle, Daniel Craig, Nick Knight and architect David Chipperfield.

ADDRESS

KILGOUR, no. 8 Savile Row, London W1S 3PE. Tel. +44 207 734 6905. www.8savilerow.com

MAURICE SEDWELL:
THE PROFESSOR

HISTORY

There can be no other firm on Savile Row that has changed its character so completely than Maurice Sedwell. Established in 1938 by the eponymous tailor, Maurice Sedwell was what present MD Andrew Ramroop calls "very much a bread and butter tailor" who brought a clientele weighted towards businessmen and captains of industry to his shop at no. 9 Savile Row. After Sedwell served his country during WWII, he established a roaring trade in demob suits from his Berners Street shop, then moved the firm to Savile Row in 1963. Mr. Sedwell's style wasn't as grand or expensive as his neighbors on the Row and this may have attracted pragmatic customers to the house who didn't want the hauteur and formality of the older firms. Mr. Sedwell was essentially a salesman who talked the same language as his business-based customers. He undercut his older neighboring houses and sold suits that were no more nor less than classic Savile Row.

Trinidad-born Andrew Ramroop arrived at Huntsman as a teenager having served his apprenticeship in Trinidad from the tender age of 13. He told the BBC "I had always heard that Savile Row had the finest

tailors in the world and I naturally aspired to the finest." His path to
Maurice Sedwell's door was, however, unusual. He was already a skilled
tailor but aspired to be a front-of-house cutter. In order to learn his trade
he chose to pay his way through the London College of Fashion, working
first as an alterations tailor on King's Road and then as a technician for
students in the years above him at college. It was no surprise that he won
the London region schools training competition. At LCF he attended
master classes given by Savile Row legends such as Harry Helman.
Helman, a name that has faded from Savile Row, is worth a brief detour.
Soho-born brothers Harry and Burt Helman were the quintessential
Jewish tailors who set up shop in 1929 and went on to dress royals,
members of the Rothschild family, Muhammad Ali, James Fox, Lord
King and Terence Stamp, not to mention the Jewish establishment. Their
shop at no. 10 Savile Row was next door to Maurice Sedwell who traded
at no. 9, upstairs from dapper dandy Bobby Valentine. Though Helman
closed its doors in 1989, Harry Helman is still remembered by the likes of
Edward Sexton and Malcolm Plews as the original godfather of the Row.
On graduating from LCF, Ramroop found Savile Row wasn't ready for a
colored front-of-house cutter. It is to Maurice Sedwell's credit that he
saw Ramroop's talent and hired him in 1974. Ramroop had seen Tommy
Nutter pushing bespoke tailoring towards flamboyance and fashion and,
in the Nutter tradition, wore his own unique style of bespoke suit in the
shop that interested the customers and intrigued Mr. Sedwell. Though
he didn't retire until 1988, even then Maurice Sedwell was winding
down. He saw Ramroop's sharp cuts bring in the Tory cabinet grandees
from 1979 when Margaret Thatcher became Prime Minister. At one
point, practically half the cabinet members were wearing Maurice
Sedwell suits. Mr. Sedwell must have been surprised to see his business
romping to the front of the field as tailor to the new establishment.
A photograph of the rotund, avuncular Mr. Sedwell still stands on the
cutting table in Maurice Sedwell. He "retired" in 1988 but could often
be seen holding court in the shop that bore his name until his death in
1991. Richard Walker relates that "Rhymester and homespun
philosopher Maurice Sedwell reflects back on fifty years of making the
ungainly look great." In tailoring as in boxing, "it's the legs that go
first," he finds. On Savile Row quality (he says) "Some are better than
others, but charlatans don't last long . . . It's all soul, this business."

It is a sentiment professor Ramroop would endorse. In 1976, Ramroop had become a part time tutor of pattern cutting, fitting and tailoring at LCF. His teaching career lasted a further twelve years, and he was made professor in 2004. The previous year he won the Black Enterprise Award as International Businessman of the Year, and in 2005 he won the Excellence award sponsored by the Mayors of London development agency. Maurice Sedwell Ltd. also won the highest accolade at the World Congress of Master Tailors held in Treviso, Italy. He inaugurated the Professor Andrew Ramroop Prize for outstanding graduate at Harvard's African/American Department.

THE COMPANY TODAY

"One-on-one personal care and a dedication to craftsmanship is the rock upon which Maurice Sedwell's reputation was built, and is still the hallmark of the company today," says professor Ramroop. The professor upholds the Savile Row dictate that the street is strictly by appointment and not merely a shopping street. 90% of the bespoke suits crafted by the house are cut using British worsted cloth, and an average of ninety hours of skilled labor are put into each suit before its advance fitting. Maurice Sedwell has customers in over fifty countries and professor Ramroop has been particularly successful in taking Savile Row tailoring to Russia. It is professor Ramroop's ambition to form a Savile Row tailoring academy on the street and revive the principal of learning from the masters.

HOUSE STYLE

"Hand cut, hand tailored, handsome" says Andrew Ramroop, whose personal touch can be seen in ingenious detail and subtle innovations, though all within the bounds of great tradition and impeccable taste.

FAMOUS/INFAMOUS CUSTOMERS

Like his predecessor Maurice Sedwell, Mr. Ramroop does not divulge his customers' names. But it was a Maurice Sedwell blazer that Diana Princess of Wales wore for her infamous *Panorama* interview.

ADDRESS

MAURICE SEDWELL LTD., 19 Savile Row, London W1S 3PP. Tel. +44 207 734 0824. www.savilerowtailor.com

NORTON & SONS:
MODERN BRITISH TAILORING

HISTORY

In 1821 Walter Grant Norton opened his tailor's shop on the Strand.
Little is recorded of the founder or his salad days as a city tailor. In
1859, Norton & Sons had moved to Lombard Street at the heart of
London's financial quarter. Guv'nor George James Norton was
granted the freedom of the City of London for his services to
tailoring, so clearly the business was both prestigious and recognized
by the Victorian establishment as comparable to Savile Row. Emperor
Wilhelm I of Prussia certainly thought so, conferring on the firm his
Royal Warrant after having been introduced to Norton & Sons in
1862 when he visited London for the marriage of Louis IV, Grand
Duke of Hesse and Princess Alice, the daughter of Queen Victoria
and mother of the ill-fated last Tsarina of Russia.

Thanks to Queen Victoria's prolific children and grandchildren, the
Prussian House of Hohenzollern and the monarchies of Spain, Greece,
Romania, Denmark and Russia were all intertwined by marriage. As
the matriarch of Europe's monarchies, Queen Victoria drew her
extended family to London and hence to its tailors such as Norton &

Sons. The nineteenth century was an era characterized by men of action who were either dressed in military, equestrian or court clothing. Norton & Sons specialized in tailoring to the young and sporting gentlemen. The Norton cut was for dashing, adventurous men and took them to the far reaches of the British Empire (practically one third of the globe).

With a strong tradition in tailoring to colonial Africa, India and the near East, Norton & Sons developed an expertise in lightweight touring and safari clothing. Norton's clothes were present when Lord Carnarvon opened Tutankhamon's tomb in the Valley of Kings in Egypt, when Stanley found Dr. Livingstone at Ujiji and when the Marquis de Vogue (the celebrated nineteenth-century French historian and traveler) undertook his "Voyage en Syrie et en Palestine." Other robust and rugged gentlemen drawn to the Norton cut included Baron Manfred von Richthofen (the World War I German fighter ace better known as the Red Baron) and Colonel Chuck Yeager (the first man to break the sound barrier in his supersonic plane the Bell X-1).

Norton & Sons arrived on at no. 16 Savile Row in 1981 after a long spell at 20 Conduit Street. The current shop is one of very few of the original houses laid down by the Burlington Estate and has, over the years, been home to many eminent individuals including Sir Henry Banks, Count Welderen and Sir Benjamin Brodie. The business remained in the Norton family until the retirement of Grant Norton in 1963 when control passed to master tailor John Granger.

John Granger had trained under Sir Hardy Amies, the couturier at no. 14 Savile Row. He cut prototypes for Hardy Amies's early men's ready-to-wear collections and made suits for Amies himself. When Granger took over at Norton & Sons, Sir Hardy became the firm's most prolific customer. In one particularly good year in the seventies Mr. Amies purchased eighteen suits, three jackets, seven trousers, two overcoats and a Marcella dress vest in addition to uniforms for the staff at no. 14. Under John Granger the firm continued to grow its business in the USA. Norton & Sons tailors would travel twice a year aboard the Queens Mary and Elizabeth. Granger and his American wife Irit increased the USA diary to six visits per year.

At the behest of Irit Granger—who always traveled with her

husband—Norton & Sons dug deeper than the usual Savile Row circuit (Washington, New York, Boston, Dallas, San Francisco and LA), exploring pockets of wealth and civilization in Raleigh (North Carolina), the Hamptons and Newport. *The Savile Row Story* records that Granger's philosophy was "we still sell British tradition but you have to change—business changes, attitudes change, everything changes." *The Savile Row Story* describes no. 16 under the Grangers as "exuding the cute coziness of a yuppy clothing boutique in the Hamptons." In fact, an East Hampton shop was the first to market the Norton Field Range, a collection of costly ready-made outfits for the American hunting/shooting/fishing set.

The Grangers' travel itinerary for autumn 1983 showed the firm visiting eighteen cities in the USA with additional trips to continental Europe. If any firm on the Row has a totally dynamic, international reputation then Norton & Sons' is well deserved. In the seventies Norton & Sons incorporated the famous old Savile Row firms of J. Hoare & Co. and E. Tautz & Sons, the noted sporting tailors who created the Tautz Lapel. Tautz dressed the eminent if long forgotten A. J. Drexel Biddle who was considered America's best-dressed man in his day. John Granger's son Nicholas sold the firm in 2005 to current director Patrick Grant.

THE COMPANY TODAY

Today Norton & Sons make clothes for three of Europe's royal families as well as two USA presidents and other heads of state. Norton & Sons was and is popular with the hunting, shooting and fishing fraternity making a fine range of shooting jackets, safari suits and field coats cut with the requisite back pleats, bellows pockets and leather patching that each sport demands. But under new guv'nor Patrick Grant, Norton & Sons is acquiring quite a reputation for cutting simply elegant suits for town and country using cloths from the most exclusive mills in Yorkshire and Scotland.

In 2005 Norton & Sons was put up for sale and acquired by Grant, a 34-year-old graduate of New College, Oxford, grandson of a Galashiels yarn spinner, and the youngest guv'nor on the Row. At Grant's prompting, Norton & Sons has cleared the decks of Hamptons style and replaced it with a clean, simple aesthetic that—

but for a well-placed leather sofa and the odd tailor's dummy—is neat, clean and spare to the point of minimal. A younger clientele appreciates the brisk simplicity of the Norton cut.

HOUSE STYLE

Grant describes the Norton cut as "neat, simple and elegant. We are proud to make beautiful, robust clothes for the dashing Englishman at large."

ROYAL WARRANT

Master tailor and head cutter John Kent holds the Royal Warrant for H.R.H. the Duke of Edinburgh.

FAMOUS/INFAMOUS CUSTOMERS

H.I.H. Kaiser Wilhelm of Prussia, Henry Stanley, Wilfred Thesiger, the Marquis de Vogue, Baron Manfred von Richthofen, Cary Grant, Frank Sinatra, Bing Crosby, Gary Cooper, Sir Hardy Amies, Alfred Hitchcock, David Niven.

ADDRESS

NORTON & SONS, 16 Savile Row, London W1S 3PL. Tel. +44 207 437 0829. www.nortonandsons.co.uk

THE MAVERICKS

DOUGLAS HAYWARD:
THE ENTERTAINER

HISTORY

Charmer Douglas "Dougie" Hayward was arguably the first superstar bespoke tailor that London produced in the swinging sixties. Tommy Nutter may have dominated Savile Row later in the decade, but it was Hayward with his shop in chic Mount Street in Mayfair—round the corner from jet set playgrounds Aspinall's, Annabel's and Harry's Bar—who took the sixties celebrity circuit by storm. Hayward didn't just dress the stars: he socialized with them and was a fixture on the Barbados-Mustique circuit along with pals David Bailey, Lord Litchfield and the Princess Margaret set of *louche* aristocrats and movie stars.

Not bad for a cockney lad whose mum was a factory worker and whose dad washed London busses in an East End depot. In a 1968 interview, Hayward revealed that his creative flair was inherited from his Dad who would "cultivate a huge piece of topiary over his front garden gate that would have been more at home in the grounds of Blenheim Palace." Hayward was encouraged to leave school at 15 and learn a trade. The way out of the working class ghetto pointed in two directions: soccer and bespoke tailoring. Hayward chose tailoring because he thought it was the quickest way of getting bespoke suits on the cheap. Also, as he said, "there was a distinction between a factory job that needed an overall and one where you kept your hands clean. I wanted clean hands." Like his contemporary Edward Sexton, Hayward's thick cockney accent didn't endear him to Savile Row and while Sexton found an apprenticeship at Kilgour, French & Stanbury, Hayward found work at a tailor's shop in Shepherd's Bush.

Whether a case of luck or foresight, Hayward was in place just as the BBC had built their new television studios at Shepherd's Bush. Hayward's daughter Polly recalls that Dougie would stalk emerging TV stars such as Spike Milligan, Peter Sellers and Eric Sykes as they were leaving the BBC and offer to make them suits. If they liked what they saw they could pay for it. His business was proof that the inhibiting old class structure was twitching its final throes. "There was no way I could have done it in England at any other time," said Hayward.

At this time in his life, Hayward entered into a partnership with Fulham Road tailor Dimi Major. Major is best remembered as the tailor who made diminutive BBC TV star Ronnie Corbett (of *The Two Ronnies*) all of the loudly checked blazers and matching tartan trews that became Corbett's signature trademark. By now, Hayward had his own book of burgeoning sixties TV stars and he was ready for a move into the West End. His choice of Mount Street was an astute one. Alongside King's Road, Mayfair was the hottest district in sixties London. Imagine a more posh, ineffably groovy Austin Powers, baby. Hayward lived above the shop and it's fair to say he gained a reputation as a Mayfair romeo. He hung out with the handsomest, coolest men of his era: Terence Stamp, Patrick Lichfield (the Queen's cousin), Bryan Forbes, Roger Moore and Michael Caine. The theory that Hayward inspired the cockney Alfie played by Caine in the eponymous 1966 film is not without a grain of truth. Working class was considered sexy for the first time, and Hayward was the smoothest bit of rough in Mayfair.

Hayward went on to dress Stamp in the film *Modesty Blaise* (1966), co-starring Monica Vitti, as well as Peter Lawford (brother-in-law of

the late JFK) in *Salt & Pepper* (1968). His most famous fashion
moment was in Caine's 1969 film *The Italian Job*, co-starring Noel
Coward: one of the most influential fashion films for men of all time.
The scene where Caine is briefing his criminal gang in London about
the proposed Italian gold bullion raid is justifiably famed for
Hayward's sharp white shirt/white tie and dark, waisted skinny suit
combination appearing thirty-five years before Hedi Slimane
rediscovered the aesthetic for Dior Homme.

The sixties didn't end on December 31, 1969. Those good times
rolled well into the seventies as the success of Nutter and Sexton
demonstrated down the road in Savile Row. Hayward had been
dressing the dapper young James Bond star Roger Moore off-screen
for many years when the star became a tax exile in 1978 after
Moonraker, decamping to live in the South of France. With his time
limited in London, Moore needed a tailor who could travel to him
and tailor his 007 suits for *For Your Eyes Only*. Hayward was no
stranger to the Côte D'Azur and readily obliged.

Even geeky James Bond fanatics tend to agree that Hayward's tenure
as bespoke tailor to James Bond was probably when the spy looked
his most suave. Former Bond tailor Cyril Castle had tended to dress
Moore in wide-lapelled sports jackets, slacks and safari suits in an
attempt to keep Bond in the swing of men's fashion. Hayward took
Bond back to the three-piece navy pinstripe city suit, but cut it in his
signature slim fit with sharp, stark shirt and tie combinations. The
look did not and has not dated and Brioni has revisited the Hayward
style for Daniel Craig's 2007 007 debut *Casino Royale*.

Dougie Hayward continued to make regular trips to Hollywood,
New York, the Côte D'Azur and Mustique as much to catch up with
old friends as to fit bespoke suits. When *The Savile Row Story*'s
Richard Walker caught up with him in Mustique, he found
Hayward in pensive mood. "In ten years' time there's not going to
be anyone left . . . unless someone faces up to the facts . . . The
tailors that are left will have to find machines to do the boring jobs
and leave them with the creative work. That is what everyone is
holding out against."

Hayward's solution was to bring a dozen Savile Row tailors together
to buy a building and operate a joint office and workshop. "The style,

the individuality a person comes to you for, that wouldn't change," he told Walker, "you would still impose your own look on it, but without all the mundane, boring stuff." Now, almost twenty years later, this is an idea that Ozwald Boateng is promoting to his neighbors on Savile Row. One of the last projects that Hayward worked on was as an unofficial consultant for Ralph Lauren's "purple label" suiting concept.

THE COMPANY TODAY

Douglas Hayward is now the *éminence grise* of the firm, and the lucky or loyal customer may find him in the shop dispensing advice about his bespoke Hayward suit. He still lives above 95 Mount Street and receives visitors such as Michael Caine, Michael Parkinson and his former cutter Henry Rose in a leather armchair that stands like a throne in the front of the shop. Hayward is a lion in winter and one gets the impression his life of jet setting and hi-jinx may have looked more fun than it actually proved to be. His right hand man, Audie Charles, continues to run the shop with a combination of brisk efficiency and charm. The Hayward Classics accessories collection is designed by Audie Charles. Hayward's daughter Polly has put her directorial and scriptwriting career in LA and New York on hold to return to London and steer Hayward into the uncharted waters of a future without the patriarch in charge. Polly Hayward is already working on a made-to-measure block to compliment the bespoke service and pursuing a younger generation of bright young things; most of whom she grew up with and socializes with now as her father did with their parents in the good old days. Watch this space for Hayward: The Next Generation.

HOUSE STYLE

Slim and sharp as a knife-edge is the Hayward cut. The shop still puts together shirts, ties and separates to compliment the bespoke service with as sure an eye as Dougie Hayward's in 1969 when he dressed Caine in *The Italian Job*. Under Polly, Hayward may be the firm that finally fulfils Savile Row's promise to tailor for women as successfully and with as much dash as it does for men.

FAMOUS/INFAMOUS CUSTOMERS

Sir Michael Caine, Rex Harrison, David Niven, Sam Spiegel, Sammy Cahn, Bryan Forbes, Sammy Davis Jr., Peter Lawford, Terence Stamp, Sir Roger Moore, Oliver Reed, Michael Winner, Jackie Stewart, Clint Eastwood, Steve McQueen, Joan Collins, Lord Lichfield, Lord Hanson, Lord Hambleden, Lord Olivier, Richard Burton, Lord "Gordy" White, the Duke of Abercorn, Sir John Mills, David Bailey, Lord Snowdon, Vidal Sassoon, Kirk Douglas, Tony Bennett, Charlton Heston, James Coburn, Michael Parkinson, Nigel Havers, Hugh Grant, A.A. Gill, Ben Goldsmith, James Ruben.

ADDRESS

DOUGLAS HAYWARD, 95 Mount Street, London W1K 2TA. Tel. +44 207 499 5574.

Rock on Tommy

He revolutionised Savile Row,
and dressed everyone from
the Beatles to Bianca Jagger.
Why does no one remember
the great Tommy Nutter?
By Stuart Husband

EDWARD SEXTON: SARTORIAL SCULPTOR

HISTORY

Like Lennon and McCartney, Edward Sexton's name is inextricably linked with the late Tommy Nutter. The shop this dynamic duo opened together on Saint Valentine's Day in 1969—Nutters of Savile Row—revolutionized the Row. "This place was dying on its feet and he (Nutter) was a bit of a whirlwind that blew through us and put us back on the map," Henry Poole chairman Angus Cundey commented. If pretty, witty Tommy Nutter was the face of the house, its skilled hands belonged to master cutter Edward Sexton.

Sexton was a mere 16 years old when he began his apprenticeship at Kilgour, French & Stanbury with the legendary Fred Stanbury as his mentor. Ferociously ambitious, he spent his days learning from the master of bespoke tailoring and his nights at the London College of Fashion. In 1967 he joined Donaldson, Williams & Ward in the Burlington Arcade where Sexton cut for customers such as the royal house of Luxembourg while Tommy Nutter worked as a front-of-house junior salesman,

London was swinging in the late sixties and the puckish Nutter charmed some very influential people at clubs such as the Ad Lib where he met the Beatles' manager Brian Epstein and singer Cilla Black. Sexton was already creating the blueprint for Nutter's superstar suiting (extravagant lapels and upswept shoulders on shaped jackets twinned with flared "Oxford Bags"). Nutter wore variations on the theme at Donaldson, Williams & Ward and inspired customers to emulate the sales boy's rakish style.

With backing from Cilla Black, James Vallance White and the Beatles' record company executive Peter Brown (who was, by then, very close to Nutter), Nutters of Savile Row opened its doors in 1969. "I remember the opening party," Cilla Black told *The Independent* journalist Stuart Husband for a definitive Tommy Nutter feature, "There was Lord Montagu and Twiggy with Justin de Villeneuve and Paul McCartney and a bunch of East End gangsters." Black also recalls "huge purple candles that were penis-shaped." Nutter and Sexton were respectful of traditional bespoke tailoring but closer in age and attitude to their sparkling client list; a host of people who wanted the contemporary details that the house became famed for. The look of late sixties suiting was, according to Nutter, "a narrow suit. So one of the first things I did was to go wild with the lapels and cut them as wide as I could . . . and team this very shaped jacket with flared trousers." "The old established Savile Row tailors said they'd give us six months," says Sexton, "Well, we took off. It was the perfect time. Hair was long, ties were big, real estate was zooming and he (Tommy) did something quite revolutionary with window displays. We made a style that knocked your socks off." Nutters' was the first Savile Row tailor to pioneer the "open window," through which passersby could see chocolate carpets, mirrored walls and mad architectural salvage from a demolished stately home in Isleworth. The window displays were designed by Simon Doonan, now maestro creative director of Barneys, New York, and included such titillating tableaux as tuxedos leaping from trashcans surrounded by a chorus line of stuffed rats sporting diamond chokers. It was Nutter's whim to trim his audaciously cut tweed, tartan and checks suits in *grosgrain* or satin, and it was Sexton who made this all happen.

Nutter ruled London in a similar fashion to Halston in New York.

John and Yoko, Mick and Bianca and Lord and Lady Montagu were married in fierce white three-piece trouser suits cut with "Sexton appeal." Three of the four Beatles wore Nutter on the iconic Abbey Road album cover while society boys such as restaurateur Stewart Grimshaw (with a twenty-six-inch waist) were walking billboards for Savile Row's first superstar designer/proprietor. Tommy Nutter was a Pied Piper who led glamorous queers, peers, rock starts and royals onto the Row much to the amusement of Henry Poole's Angus Cundey and Hardy Amies.

Men's Wear magazine nailed the success of Nutters of Savile Row: "Whereas the traditional Savile Row tailor is still doing well by doing nothing to change his image, Tommy Nutter is still doing well by doing something." Banter in the workrooms of the Savile Row tailors is traditionally camp and salty. Nutter brought that vernacular onto the shop floor. All of the gay customers were given girl's names, and John Lennon was awarded the singular privilege of being the only straight man to be conferred with this honor. He was called Carol.

The party didn't last forever, and in a *coup d'état* Tommy Nutter exited the house that bore his name in 1976. Nutter called the split "messy" and the house continued without him under Edward Sexton, Roy Chittleborough and Joseph Morgan. As Sexton summed up, "Tommy is a brilliant public relations person; a charming, lovely chap and let's be honest he's done more to revive Savile Row than anybody else."

Kilgour, French & Stanbury took Nutter under its formidable wing in 1977 and he opened on the Row under his own name in the early eighties when a young Timothy Everest, John Galliano and Turnbull & Asser's current press attaché Rowland Lowe-Mackenzie joined the playpen. "He'd forgotten more than I'll ever know," says Everest. Projects such as a ready-to-wear collection for Fortnum & Mason, stage get-ups for Elton John, Jack Nicholson's costumes as the Joker in *Batman* and a license in Japan followed as Tommy Nutter slowly began to drown in a cocktail of booze, boys and, eventually, HIV. Nutter died in 1992. He was 49.

Sexton, meanwhile, made a smart move at Nutters of Savile Row by insisting on an advance deposit from bespoke customers, thus ending

the tradition of unlimited credit and cash long after delivery. By
1981 he too walked away from Nutters, opening Edward Sexton at
no. 37 Savile Row. Thus began two decades of glamour. As Richard
Walker, author of *The Savile Row Story*, says, "The quintessential
Savile Row exporter is Edward Sexton" who told the author that his
business was 85-90% export. Already well acquainted with the spider
web of glamorous gay jetsetters thanks to Tommy, Sexton embarked
on regular USA tours that took him to New York, San Francisco and
LA at around about the same time as Giorgio Armani was first
romancing Hollywood and spotting "dress the stars" potential.
Sexton was also up to speed with fashion industry marketing,
appointing a Manhattan publicist and regularly appearing in the
New York Post's "Suzy" column every time he came to town. "The
old school was so snobbish," he told the LA press. "Rather than sit on
our backsides waiting for someone to push open the door, we're much
more aware of marketing."

With a showroom on Manhattan's Upper East Side, Sexton dressed
them all: New York "walker" to Jackie Kennedy and Nancy Reagan,
the late Jerry Zipkin, Kenneth J. Lane, Bill Blass and social titans
Rupert Murdoch, George Soros and former President Gerald Ford. In
1988 he opened his first Edward Sexton shop for a ready-to-wear
interpretation of the London line in Saks Fifth Avenue. Sexton is a
pioneer for new generation tailors such as Kilgour, Ozwald Boateng,
Richard James and Timothy Everest. He is the first to admit that he
made the inevitable mistakes any pioneer must when it came to
translating bespoke philosophy into an international ready-to-wear
collection. A self-confessed perfectionist, Edward Sexton does not
compromise. He is not the first nor will he be the last to survive the
lethal cocktail of success, fame, hubris and liquor. Sexton continues to
dress the bright and beautiful in London and the USA, but has quit
Savile Row.

THE COMPANY TODAY

The self-styled "Bespoke master tailor of Knightsbridge" works from
a light-flooded first floor studio between San Lorenzo and Bruce
Oldfield on Beauchamp Place. Even from street level it's possible to
catch glimpses of Sexton's shock of white "punk pixie" hair and the

clouds of Dunhill cigarette smoke that announce he's in residence. Mr. Sexton is a great teacher of the bespoke craft and students such as a young Stella McCartney flock to his studio. When McCartney was awarded the top job at Chloe, Sexton was her tailoring mentor and developed the suiting blocks for her first Chloe catwalk collection and all subsequent shows from Beauchamp Place. Edward Sexton has seen it all, done it all and dressed them all. Unlike Tommy Nutter, he's still here.

HOUSE STYLE

The London Cut—"a little more emphasis on the shoulder, a little more expression into the chest area"—gives his suits that old Sexton appeal. He describes it thus: "A Sexton suit is of a soft construction distinguished by a high-cut armhole and rope shoulder with a distinctive collar and lapel shape and, finally, the Edward Sexton touch of a higher waist creating the taller slender silhouette whilst still remaining a very comfortable feel."

FAMOUS/INFAMOUS CUSTOMERS

John Lennon and Yoko Ono, Sir Paul and Linda McCartney, Ringo Starr, George Harrison, Brian Epstein, Cilla Black, Mick Jagger, Bianca Jagger, Eric Clapton, the Duke of Bedford, Lord Montagu of Beaulieu, Lady Bamford, Joan Collins, Twiggy, Stella McCartney, Lord Lichfield, Maggie Smith, Bill Blass, Sir Hardy Amies, Manolo Blahnik, Jack Nicholson, Jerry Zipkin.

ADDRESS

EDWARD SEXTON, 26 Beauchamp Place, London SW3 1NJ. Tel. +44 207 838 0007.

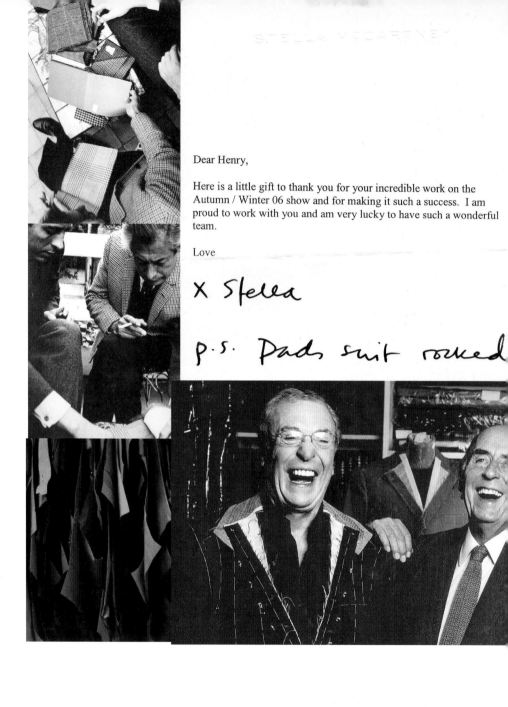

Dear Henry,

Here is a little gift to thank you for your incredible work on the Autumn / Winter 06 show and for making it such a success. I am proud to work with you and am very lucky to have such a wonderful team.

Love

X Stella

p.s. Dads suit rocked

HENRY ROSE:
THE LADIES' MAN

HISTORY

Perched on the second floor of Stella McCartney's Bruton Street townhouse, Henry Rose is responsible for cutting bespoke suits for McCartney's stellar private customers as well as his own loyal and no less glittering following. Rose started his apprenticeship in 1960 at Kilgour, French & Stanbury as a coat maker. Kilgour was and is renown for training the most talented cutters in the business. Rose supplemented his tailoring apprenticeship making overcoats, eveningwear and waistcoats at Kilgour with evening classes that taught him how to cut.

After four years, Rose was qualified to call himself a Kilgour tailor and remained in this role for a year before moving to Piccadilly-based company Chapmans. In a bold and daring move, Rose opened his first shop at the age of 19 on Meard Street in Soho (the street where fellow maverick John Pearse now plies his trade). Rose's mother had to sign the lease on the property because, at 19, he was too young to sign legal documents.

Like fellow maverick Edward Sexton, who was an undercutter and

Rose's contemporary at Kilgour, Henry Rose never sat still. The two gentlemen found themselves working at Welsh & Jeffries (then in St. James's), and while Sexton went on to form Nutters of Savile Row with Tommy Nutter in 1969, Rose went on to work for legendary seventies firms Peter Moore, Douglas Hayward, the Helman Brothers, Lew Fuirst, Bobby Valentine and Robbie Stanford. He worked with Sexton at Nutters, then again when Edward Sexton opened his eponymous shop on the Row.

Rose's wanderlust was amplified by his ambitions to work on the stage. In 1976 he won *The Scotsman* (newspaper) award at the Edinburgh Fringe Festival, and he would continue to audition, rehearse and tour for the remainder of the decade while working for the great Douglas Hayward at his Mount Street shop. Hayward was the only tailor to rival Nutter and Sexton for celebrity clientele. His great friend (former *Cosmopolitan* editor) Marcelle D'Argy Smith calls Hayward the "wittiest, sharpest dresser of all time."

As a Hayward taylor, Henry Rose would meet everyone from Kirk Douglas to Sir John Mills. Hayward was good friends with all the big beasts of British film and theater. His shop and Mount Street apartment constituted a den comparable to Annabel's or Tramp for sharp-suited starts such as Sir Michael Caine, Sir Roger Moore, Peter Sellers and the Princess Margaret set. Hayward had dressed arguably the greatest men's fashion film—*The Italian Job* (1969)—and also reinvented James Bond during Roger Moore's tenure as James 007. Rose has never lost touch with Doug Hayward, and continues to visit the great man and his daughter Polly as she revitalizes the business for 2007.

In the eighties, Rose once again opened his own shop in Soho's Kingly Street: the road parallel to Carnaby Street where the last remaining workshop dedicated to tailoring survives. In 1995 Hayward used his influence to put Rose forward as the bespoke business for the Bond Street house of Sulka (the firm responsible for Sir Noel Coward's silk dressing gowns). In 2000, Rose was invited to run Dunhill's bespoke tailoring rooms. It was at Dunhill that Henry Rose first encountered Madonna and went on to make the kilt jacket for Guy Ritchie's Scottish wedding to Madonna at Stella McCartney's instigation. The Richemont Group-owned Dunhill was—with then public relations director Joan Rolls's help—at the heart of the set for Guy Ritchie's *Lock, Stock and Two Smoking Barrels*, and thus Rose dressed the Rat Pack of British twenty-first century film.

THE COMPANY TODAY
In 2003, the Gucci Group-owned Stella McCartney opened her four-story Georgian flagship store on London's Bruton Street (also home to Matthew Williamson, Holland & Holland, Brioni and the old Hartnell showroom). McCartney, who had trained under Rose's old boss Edward Sexton, asked Rose to be her bespoke tailor-in-residence at no. 30. Henry Rose's atelier is on the second floor, next to the VIP room to which he is called on a regular basis to tailor for McCartney's profile clients. But judging from his past record as maybe the most footloose maverick tailor, it is questionable whether Rose will remain in his Bruton Street eerie for much longer.

HOUSE STYLE
One of the few bespoke tailors who understands cutting for women, Rose made a neat, sharp shooting tweed three-piece for Madonna that was subsequently photographed for *Vanity Fair*. Like Edward Sexton, he is a master of the white three-piece trouser suit for men and women. He started the vogue for girls about town to wear black or white variations on the Royal Ascot morning coat with miniskirts and heels.

FAMOUS/INFAMOUS CUSTOMERS
Madonna, Guy Ritchie, Mike Tyson, Stella McCartney, Sir Paul McCartney, Gwyneth Paltrow, Neil Tennant, Padma Rushdie, Chrissie Hynde, Lulu, Olivia Harrison, Barbara Bach, Grace Jones, Kelis, Kirsten Dunst, Pamela Anderson, Alasdhair Willis, Jake Chapman, Graham Rust, Nadja Swarovski, Jason Flemyng, Peter Jones, Jonathan Meades, Patsy Kensit, Sir Roger Moore, Alec Guinness, Sir John Mills, Michael Parkinson, Sir Sean Connery, François-Henri Pinault, David Frost, Sir Michael Caine, Joe Cole, Trevor Sinclair, Paul Getty, Victor Borge.

ADDRESS
HENRY ROSE at Stella McCartney, 30 Bruton Street, London W1J 6LG. Tel. +44 207 518 3114. www.henryrose.co.uk

MEASURING AND FIGURATION

9 HEIGHT
Measure to nearest 1" and give measure in FEET and INCHES.

10 NAPE TO WAIST MEASURE
Follow contour of body from Nape to Natural Waist Position.

11 JACKET LENGTH MEASURE
Place end of tape at the collar seam (NAPE) and down the back to the length required.

12 HALF BACK MEASURE
Tension jacket back and Measure from sleeve seam to sleeve seam and HALVE THE RESULT i.e. 16" across back ÷ 6" HALF BACK.

13 CROWN TO CUFF MEASURE
Place Tape end at CENTRE OF SLEEVE CUFF at required length and measure up to CROWN OF SLEEVE (Highest point of Sleeve)

FORWARD SHOULDERS & PROM BLADES
The jacket will crease on the foreparts from the neck point across to the base of the front scye.
R

RS or RSS

DROP LEFT SHOULDER
Button and buttonhole mis-aligned. Fullness at left back scye.
LS or LSS

SLOPING SHOULDERS/ LONG NECK
Fullness at both scyes. An abnormal amount of shirt collar will be showing above the jacket collar.
X or XX

EASY SCYES
The jacket will be tight in the armholes creating creasing over biceps.
ES

ERECT CHEST
Jacket will appear longer at the back and tight on the seat. Half back area will appear full and half back measure will be less than normal for chest measure.
P or PP

FULL CHEST
Jacket will appear longer at the back and tight on the seat. A gap will also appear on inside edge of lapels when jacket is buttoned.
W or WW

SWAY BACK
Jacket stands off seat but hemline is parallel to floor.
G only

15 JACKET/VEST CHEST MEASURE
Place the tape around the chest, keeping it well up and underneath the arms. Tape should be over the shoulder blades and parallel to the ground. Make sure the measurement is taken with the body relaxed.

16 JACKET/VEST WAIST MEASURE
Place tape on the NATURAL WAIST POSITION (at naval) - this could be over the narrowest part of the waist or over a prominent stomach.

24 OUTSIDE LEG (side seam)
Measure right leg. Measure from top of waistband down sideseam to required length. NOTE: Mentally check RISE (body of Trouser) by subtracting inside leg from outside leg. If answer is LESS THAN 10" CHECK MEASURES.

25 TROUSER FIGURATION
Prominent Seat
Code I
Low front waist (Corpulent figure)
Code L

JOHN PEARSE
6 Meard Street London W1V 3HR
Telephone: 0171 434 0738
VAT No. 466 4423 36
Fax 0171 287 3862

"Stephen believes in good manners, but he could verbally destroy you anytime he chose."

JOHN PEARSE:
SAVILE ROW ON ACID

HISTORY

A teenager on the burgeoning Mod scene in the early sixties in London, a young John Pearse knocked on Henry Poole's door in Cork Street and asked for a job. The 15-year-old kid wanted to know how to cut the then-fashionable mohair Mod suiting. As he told Max Decharne, author of *King's Road: The Rise and Fall of the Hippest Street in the World*, "They told me to wait and as I was sitting there David Niven walked in looking debonair to pick up some suits. I thought 'this is great. I'm going to meet the stars.'" Poole's sent Pearse round the corner to Hawes & Curtis on Dover Street where he became an apprentice coat maker.

"We were upstairs in the workroom which was like Fagin's den," recalled Pearce. "Everyone was very young and it had quite a good ambience for learning the craft. Those guys were all kind of Mod-y as well, even though they were making the Duke of Edinburgh's kit or the King of Thailand's stuff. It gave me good grounding for the flamboyance to come."

Hawes & Curtis sent Pearse's father a telegram in 1961 that he has to

this day: "I am sure he will make a first class tailor if he continues to show the interest and keenness which he has done so far." Instead of continuing his training at Hawes & Curtis, Pearse quit and went on the road, traveling in Europe. He returned from St. Tropez and Spain in 1965 and met Nigel Waymouth and Sheila Cohen (who called herself Sheila Troy). The unholy alliance that formed the sixties' most notorious boutique—Granny Takes a Trip—was born.
"Grannys" opened before Christmas 1965 and sold vintage clothes collected by Troy and recut by Savile Row-trained Pearse. "We were the first bisexual boutique," says Pearse. "What appealed to us was Aubrey Beardsley and the Victorians . . . so we were all doomed Romantics at the time. Not 'New Romantics' Romantics. So that was the influence . . . art nouveau," Pearse told Decharne. Actually the influence was art nouveau and LSD.
Both people and product fell apart at Grannys on a regular basis. Pearse called the skin-tight velvet Byron breeches he cut "tattered troubadour pants" because they invariably split in five minutes. LSD, the hallucinogenic drug, was not yet criminalized in the UK and Grannys was literally and figuratively a trip. Jimi Hendrix, Ossie Clark, the Beatles, the Rolling Stones, T-Rex, Cream and the Who were all devotees of Pearse's psychedelic shirts, William Morris tapestry jackets cut from Liberty print cloth and (later) his James Dean revival "Jet Rink" fifties-cut jackets.
Antonioni swung by and bought the dress that Veruschka wears in the iconic poster for *Blow-Up*. T-Rex lead singer Marc Bolan helped to paint the famous Mae West window at Grannys and released a single named after the store that Pearse considered twee. Terence Stamp, Andy Warhol, Monica Vitti and Bardot found their way to Grannys, as did (rather bizarrely) author Salman Rushdie, who rented a room upstairs and recalled:
"You went into Grannys through a heavily beaded curtain and were instantly blinded. The air was heavy with incense and patchouli oil and also the aromas of what the police called 'certain substances.' Psychedelic music, big on feedback, terrorized your eardrums. After a time you became aware of a low purple glow in which you could make out a few motionless shapes. These were probably clothes for sale. You didn't like to ask."

JOHN PEARSE — 167 —

The crunch came in 1968, when Pearse found an abandoned 1947
Dodge motor car in Notting Hill, chopped it in half and stuck it
through the window at Grannys in homage to Claes Oldenburg's
Lovers in the Back Seat of a Dodge. Punches were thrown with
Waymouth keeping the shop and Pearse keeping their band.
"Neither of us did any good after that . . . " Pearse said with a smile.
In 1969 Pearse shed his skin and took a bit part in Tony
Richardson's film version of Nabokov's *Laughter in the Dark*. He'd
been in Italy and returned to London inspired by Fellini's *Dolce vita*
(1960). Pearse became Richardson's assistant at the Royal Court
Theater in Sloane Square at the opposite end of King's Road to
Grannys. Of this period in his life, Pearse says he "quit the theater
and never held a proper job again."
The Nouvelle Vague in France, Fellini in Italy and Warhol in New
York inspired Pearse to make his directorial debut with *Moviemaker*
(1971) produced by Michael White. It was a requiem for the "granny
takes a trip" generation that Pearse directed and starred in. Film
would preoccupy Pearce for another decade, and he would abandon
London for Rome before he came full circle and returned to tailoring
in 1985 with his shop on Soho's Meard Street.

THE COMPANY TODAY
Pearse is a familiar sight cycling around W1 looking more like one of
Harry Potter's eccentric magical schoolmasters than a
pioneer/survivor of the King's Road LSD scene in the sixties and an
iconoclastic filmmaker. His salon on one of Soho's finest Georgian
streets (Meard Street) is the perfect location for passing trade en route
to *louche* Soho media clubs the Groucho, Soho House, Blacks and the
Colony Rooms.

HOUSE STYLE
Pearse is a bespoke tailoring terrorist who has been known on
occasion to splash gold paint—Jackson Pollock style—at a bespoke
suit, cut a blazer from antique tapestry in homage to his William
Morris print jackets from the "Granny" days or fashion a navy
pinstripe three-piece from denim out of sheer perversity, having never
worn it in his youth. Supremely unimpressed by the famous faces he

apparently fails to recognize half the time, Pearse holds court in his shop as and when he wants to; rarely giving away his exceedingly curious past as the psychedelic tailor of Granny Takes a Trip.

FAMOUS/INFAMOUS CUSTOMERS

The Beatles, Ossie Clark, Jimi Hendrix, Veruschka, John Paul Getty, Anita Pallenberg, Brigitte Bardot, David Hockney, Mick Jagger, Malcolm McLaren, Bob Dylan, Damien Hirst, Will Self, Robbie Williams, Stephen Fry, Sebastian Horsley, Seal.

ADDRESS

JOHN PEARSE, 6 Meard Street, Soho, London W1F OEG. Tel. +44 207 434 0730. www.johnpearse.co.uk

City of Westminster

entlemen

LONDON EYE

ONLY 50P

The Capital's
Best Value
Entertainment
Guide

Clubs
Music
Film
Style
Events
Sport

The Best
Dressed Man in Town
Bespoke Tailor Mark Powell

+ MICKY HAZZARD

7-Day
TV
Guide

MARK POWELL:
EASTEND GANGSTER NO. 1

HISTORY

Eastender born and bred, Mark Powell's rise as arguably the first new generation bespoke tailor after Tommy Nutter was a case of right time and right place. He rattled off a quick succession of youth cult looks before he'd even hit puberty, with adventures as a suedehead, rockabilly and soul boy before landing at Italian import shop Washington Tremlett on Conduit Street as a very style-wise teenager. In the early eighties he introduced an in-house bespoke service at Robot (a fifties suit and shoe specialist). He was only 24 when in 1984 he opened Powell & Co. in Soho's Archer Street, selling deadstock suits from the forties and fifties discovered in a warehouse in Stoke Newington (North London).

The Mark Powell aesthetic evolved from the original 1949 neo-Edwardian "teddy boy" suiting that he purified into a four-button suit, big knotted tie, shirt with rounded, starched detachable collar, pearl stick pin, waistcoat and Balmoral boots or spats. He described the look as "not authentic . . . more what you might see on Peter Cushing in a Hammer (horror) film." Eastend gangster thugs the

Kray Twins (who Powell eventually dressed in prison) and classic Hollywood gangsters of the thirties such as George Raft and James Cagney further honed the stylized neo-Edwardian look. It was Powell's ability to remix his influences that saved the tailor from being pigeonholed. The first generation Mod look of the late fifties/early sixties was a particularly precise moment in fashion borrowed by the cult film *Absolute Beginners* starring Patsy Kensit (who Powell dressed).

Powell opened his first pure bespoke atelier on Soho's D'Arblay Street in 1991 at the height of the acid jazz movement and began dressing gents like George Michael, David Bowie, Bryan Ferry and Mick Jagger. A young Ozwald Boateng modeled Mark Powell bespoke before going on to establish his own Savile Row bespoke tailoring business. In 1997 Powell was invited to New York to dress George Clooney as Thomas Jefferson and Harrison Ford as Abraham Lincoln for the prestigious presidential covers of *George Magazine* edited by the late John Kennedy Junior. Incidentally, Powell was in New York at a Paul Smith party with Kennedy Jr. discussing a potential New York fashion show the week before Kennedy Jr. and his wife Carolyn were killed in a plane crash en route to Martha's Vineyard on July 16, 1999.

Another Mark Powell fashion moment came at the turn of the twenty-first century when, in 2000, Powell made the clothes for the movie *Gangster No. 1* featuring Paul Bettany and David Thewliss. Though he did not design the costumes for *Lock, Stock and Two Smoking Barrels*, the film directed by Madonna's husband Guy Ritchie borrowed heavily from Mark Powell's bespoke gangster aesthetic. Though Boateng and Richard James have brought the new generation aesthetic to the Row, it is Mark Powell who is the missing link between Tommy Nutter and the new Savile Row tailor/designers.

THE COMPANY TODAY

Powell remains loyal to Soho and trades from a fourth floor eerie on Brewer Street soaring above the seediness of the Shadow Lounge, Madame Jo-Jos and Too-2-Much (formerly Raymond's Revue Bar). Diamond tiepin still sparkling and favorite Berluti shoes fashioned into a near-stiletto spike, Powell is straight out of a Jake Arnott cult sixties Soho gangster novel. Arguably the first celebrity tailor of our day and age, Powell brilliantly styled Naomi Campbell in sharp suits, shirts and ties for the first of her many court appearances, and continues to dress new generation British film stars such as Daniel Radcliffe (Harry Potter) for the London and New York premiers of *Harry Potter and the Goblet of Fire* (a green velvet Regency-collared frock coat and a blue one-button mohair suit with shawl collar respectively) and Paul Bettany in sharp suits with killer details such as the Powell gauntlet cuff appropriated by Gucci. In 2005 Usher commissioned a double-breasted dinner suit and a Donegal tweed "Oxford bags" look for the short film that accompanied the video, *Caught Up*. Mark Powell's bespoke business operates between London and New York, and Powell launched a ready-to-wear line (Mark Powell London) at Pitti Uomo in July 2006. It currently sells at Liberty in London and in Japan.

HOUSE STYLE

All bespoke suiting is inevitably nostalgic because, let's face it, one isn't going to spend an average £3,000 on a bespoke suit that will be markedly out of fashion within a season. So Mark Powell's knowledge of the great decades of twentieth century men's style are totally appropriate in the world of bespoke tailoring. Powell refines the silhouette—be that twenties' Brideshead fop, thirties' Manhattan gangster, fifties' Ted or sixties' Soho spivvy Mod—to make it relevant to twenty-first century boys.

FAMOUS/INFAMOUS CUSTOMERS

Morrisey, Harrison Ford, George Clooney, Naomi Campbell, Alan Rickman, Dan MacMillan, Usher, Goldie, George Michael, Bianca Jagger, Daniel Radcliffe (Harry Potter), Ian Wright, Frank Lampard, David Bowie, Mick Jagger, Bryan Ferry.

ADDRESS

MARK POWELL, 12 Brewer Street, Soho, London W1F OSF. Tel. +44 207 287 5498.
www.markpowellbespoke.co.uk

ON THE ROW

Jude Law at the premier of *The Talented Mr. Ripley*,
London, 1999. Tailor Kilgour
© Camera Press/Gary Calton

Portrait of George III's coronation robes, 1761, now kept in the court
dress collection at Kensington Palace, London. Tailor Ede & Ravenscroft
From Una Campbell, *Robes of the Realm: 300 Years of Ceremonial
Dress*. London: Ede & Ravenscroft Ltd., 1989

Marlene Dietrich in white tie and top hat in *Morocco*, USA, 1930, director Josef von Sternberg. During the thirties, Dietrich was a frequent customer of tailor Anderson & Sheppard
© SNAP Photo Library/GraziaNeri

Prince William in a postcard produced by the London Postcard Company. Tailor Gieves & Hawkes

Cover for the Beatles' album *Abbey Road*, Apple, 1969.
Photo Iain MacMillan, design Peter Blake. For John
Lennon, Ringo Star and Paul McCartney, tailor Nutters
of Savile Row

James Clyde, a page at Queen Elizabeth II's coronation,
London, June 2, 1953. Photo Norman Parkinson. Tailor
Henry Poole & Co.
From Martin Harrison, ed., *Parkinson: Photographs
1935–1990*. London: Conran Octopus, 1994

Beatles   strisce pedonali (da tempo due

Michael Caine in *The Italian Job*, UK, 1969,
director Peter Collinson. Tailor Douglas Hayward
© Photo12/GraziaNeri

Sammy Davis Junior with Douglas Hayword, in
London during the seventies. Photo Eve Arnold. Tailor
Douglas Hayward
Courtesy Douglas Hayward Archive

Alfred Hitchcock and Cary Grant. Grant was an iconic
Kilgour customer. Hitchcock patronized Norton & Sons
From Richard Torregrossa, *Cary Grant:
A Celebration of Style.* London: Aurum Press, 2006

The wedding of Prince Charles and the Duchess of
Cornwall, Camilla Parker-Bowles, at St. George's
Chapel, Windsor Castle, April 9, 2005. For Prince
Charles, tailor Anderson & Sheppard
© Alastair Grant/ImageForum

Lord and Lady Montagu wed in white three-piece
trouser suits tailored by Edward Sexton. Tailor Nutters
of Savile Row
Courtesy Lord and Lady Montagu

The wedding of John Lennon and Yoko Ono,
Gibraltar, March 20, 1969. White suits tailored by
Edward Sexton. Tailor Nutters of Savile Row
Courtesy Edward Sexton Archive

GeOrge

NOT JUST POLITICS AS USUAL

POWER COUPLES

MAKING IT WORK, BY AL & TIPPER GORE, BOB & LIDDY DOLE, AND OTHERS

KINKY FRIEDMAN ON **JOSEPH HELLER**

THE GEORGE INTERVIEW **MADELEINE ALBRIGHT**

BRAIN DAMAGE & THE CRIMINAL MIND BY **RICHARD DOOLING**

WHY IS GAY MARRIAGE BETTER? BY **NAOMI WOLF**

MAKE WAR NOT LOVE
WHO *WAGS THE DOG* IN POLITICS—
THE PRESS OR THE PRESS SECRETARY? BY
WILLIAM KENNEDY

02
FEBRUARY
1998
USA $2.95
CANADA
$3.95
UK £2.50

631 8

DE NIRO & HOFFMAN
TOGETHER AT LAST

GeOrge

MEN MEN MEN

THE 20 MOST FASCINATING MEN IN POLITICS

DON IMUS
ON LESBIANS, LYING & LEADERSHIP
AN INTERVIEW BY JOHN KENNEDY

25 YEARS LATER: WEIRD WATERGATE WONDERS

BEST PLACES IN AMERICA FOR MEN TO LIVE

JUNE 1997
USA $2.95
CANADA
$3.95
UK £2.50

GEORGE CLOON
DECLARA
OF INDEPENDE

TOP 10 HUNKS IN HISTORY BY ARTHUR

GeOrge

KILLER RABBITS

JANET RENO EXPOSED

EXCLUSIVE: WHITEWATER'S WEBB HUBBELL ON HIS LIFE IN PRISON

WHY THE IRA WON'T STOP SHOOTING: AN INTERVIEW WITH GERRY ADAMS BY JOHN KENNEDY

ELVIS'S STRANGE DREAMS

THE SECRET PASSIONS OF
HARRISON F
PLUS: GROVER CLEVELAND'S
AND DOG GONE! A FURRY FAREW
TO MILLIE BUSH

Robert De Niro and Dustin Hoffman. Tailor Richard James
Cover of *George*, February 1998

George Clooney as Thomas Jefferson. Tailor Mark Powell
Cover of *George*, June 1997

Harrison Ford as Abraham Lincoln. Tailor Mark Powell
Cover of *George*, August 1997

Guests of the Crown Prince Hirohito (future Emperor of
Japan): the Prince of Wales, future King Edward VIII, Prince
Kan'in, the Duke of Connaught. For the Crown Prince, tailor
Henry Poole & Co.
Courtesy Henry Poole & Co. Archive

Frank Sinatra, a devoted client of Kilgour, French &
Stansbury, in a classic black tie
From Marion Maneker, *Dressing in the Dark: Lessons in Men's
Style from the Movies*. New York: Assouline, 2002
Courtesy Everett Collection

Edward VII, Prince of Wales and future King of England,
shown in an 1860 engraving. The monarch conferred his Royal
Warrant upon Henry Poole & Co. both as Prince of Wales and
as King Edward VII
© Ann Ronan Picture/Photos12

William II (1859–1941), Kaiser of Germany and King of Prussia,
wearing an official military uniform. Tailor Norton & Sons
© Private collection/Photo12

Madonna wearing a tweed three-piece. Tailor Henry Rose
Page from "Madonna Marlene," photo Steven Daly,
Vanity Fair USA, no. 506, October 2002

Winston Churchill, portrayed in an iconographic propaganda photo
for the Second World War. Tailor Henry Poole & Co., Homburg hat
by James Lock & Co.
Courtesy Henry Poole & Co. Archive

H.M. the Queen Elisabeth II, the Queen of England, on
horseback during the annual Trooping of the Color ceremony
held in London to celebrate her birthday. Uniform by Bernard
Weatherill
From Alfred Cope, ed., *Cope's Royal Cavalcade of the Turf.*
London: Cope's Publication Ltd., 1953

Portrait of King Edward VII, with the coronation robe, 1901.
Tailor Ede & Ravenscroft
From Una Campbell, *Robes of the Realm: 300 Years of
Ceremonial Dress.* London: Ede & Ravenscroft Ltd., 1989

Pete Doherty. Tailor Richard James
Page from *Esquire*, April 2005
Courtesy Richard James Archive

Steve McQueen in *The Thomas Crown Affair*, USA, 1968,
director Norman Jewison. Tailor Douglas Hayward
From Marion Maneker, *Dressing in the Dark: Lessons in Men's
Style from the Movies*. New York: Assouline, 2002
Courtesy Everett Collection

Tyrone Power in an image from the late forties. Tailor
Anderson & Sheppard
From Marion Maneker, *Dressing in the Dark: Lessons in Men's
Style from the Movies*. New York: Assouline, 2002
Courtesy Everett Collection

Cary Grant wearing a Prince of Wales checked jacket. Tailor
Kilgour, French & Stansbury
From Richard Torregrossa, *Cary Grant: A Celebration of Style.*
London: Aurum Press, 2006

Charles Dickens, 1865.
Tailor Henry Poole & Co.
Courtesy Henry Poole & Co. Archive

Duncan Davidson and the honorable James Drummond, pages
at the coronation of Queen Elizabeth II, London, June 2, 1953.
Tailor Henry Poole & Co.
From Martin Harrison, ed., *Parkinson: Photographs
1935–1990*. London: Conran Octopus, 1994

David Bowie during a "Serious Moonlight Tour" concert in
Wembley, London, 1983. Bowie is one of Savile Row's
greatest and most prolific customers. He favors Spencer Hart,
Mark Powell and John Pearse. © Rex Features/Olycom

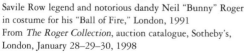

Savile Row legend and notorious dandy Neil "Bunny" Roger
in costume for his "Ball of Fire," London, 1991
From *The Roger Collection*, auction catalogue, Sotheby's,
London, January 28–29–30, 1998

Stewart Granger as George "Beau" Brummel, the father of
dandyism, in *Lord Brummel*, USA/UK, 1954, director Curtis
Bernhardt
Page from *Cloth & Clothes*, July–August 1954 Courtesy EMap
Archive, The London College of Fashion, London

Pictures: HEATHCLIFF O'MALLEY and STEPHEN LOCK

Hamish Bowles, wearing a collection of Neil "Bunny" Roger Savile Row suits bought at the Roger Estate auction, Sotheby's, London. Tailor Watson, Fargerstrom & Hughes Ltd.
Page from "Wild Card in the Fash-pack," text Hilary Alexander, photos Heathcliff O'Malley and Stephen Lock, *Daily Telegraph*, November 2, 1998

Fashion designer Ossie Clark wearing a William Morris
print tapestry jacket. Tailor John Pearse
From Paul Gorman, *The Look: Adventures in Rock & Pop
Fashion.* London: Adelita, 2006

Roger Moore in *Live and Let Die*, USA, 1973,
director Guy Hamilton. Tailor Douglas Hayward
© Photo12/GraziaNeri

Edward VII, the Prince of Wales. Tailor Henry Poole & Co.
Courtesy Henry Poole & Co. Archive

H.R.H. The Prince of Wales

Malcom McDowell, David Thewlis, Paul Bettany. Tailor Mark
Powell. Poster for *Gangster No. 1*, UK/Germany/Ireland, 2000,
director Paul McGuigan
Courtesy Mark Powell Archive

Hugh Grant. Tailor Richard James
Page from "The James Gang," photo Peter Robathan,
GQ UK, September 2000

King George V and Queen Mary in their coronation robes,
adapted from those for the coronation of his father Edward VII
and Queen Alexandra. Tailor Ede & Ravenscroft
From Una Campbell, *Robes of the Realm: 300 Years of
Ceremonial Dress*. London: Ede & Ravenscroft Ltd., 1989

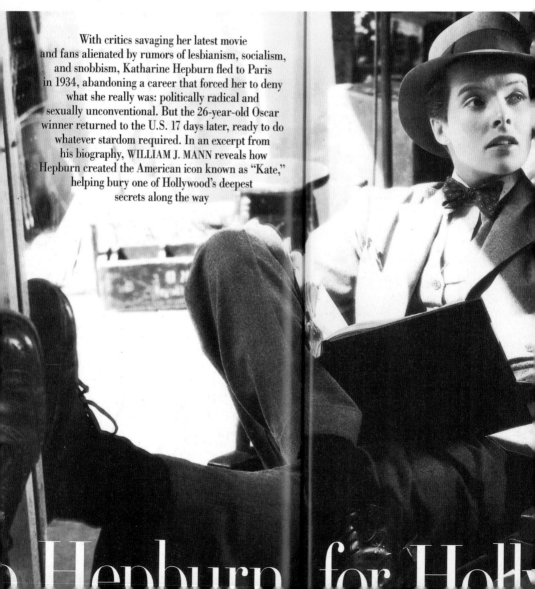

Katharine Hepburn on the set of *Sylvia Scarlett*, USA, 1935, director George Cukor. Hepburn was a faithful client of Huntsman
Page from "Too Hepburn for Hollywood," *Vanity Fair UK*, no. 554, October 2006

With critics savaging her latest movie and fans alienated by rumors of lesbianism, socialism, and snobbism, Katharine Hepburn fled to Paris in 1934, abandoning a career that forced her to deny what she really was: politically radical and sexually unconventional. But the 26-year-old Oscar winner returned to the U.S. 17 days later, ready to do whatever stardom required. In an excerpt from his biography, WILLIAM J. MANN reveals how Hepburn created the American icon known as "Kate," helping bury one of Hollywood's deepest secrets along the way

Hepburn for Holly

Queen Victoria riding in Windsor Park. Tailor Henry Poole & Co.
From Alfred Cope, ed., *Cope's Royal Cavalcade of the Turf.*
London: Cope's Publication Ltd., 1953

Gary Cooper. Tailor Anderson & Sheppard
From Marion Maneker, *Dressing
in the Dark: Lessons in Men's Style from
the Movies*. New York: Assouline, 2002
Courtesy Photofest

Fred Astaire in *Top Hat*, USA, 1935, director
Mark Sandrich. Tailor Kilgour, French &
Stansbury
From G. Bruce Boyer, *Fred Astaire Style*. New
York: Assouline, 2004

Tom Ford, London, October 2006. Photo Sølve
Sundsbø. Tailor Anderson & Sheppard
Courtesy Tom Ford

HIS MAJESTY KING GEORGE VI

King George VI. Tailor Gieves & Hawkes
From George A. Titman, ed., *Dress and Insignia Worn at
His Majesty's Court.* London: Harrison & Sons Ltd., 1937

I'm still standing.

Want strong bones?
Drinking enough
lowfat milk
now can help prevent
osteoporosis later.

got milk?

ELTON JOHN ©2000 AMERICA'S DAIRY FARMERS AND MILK PROCESSORS

Sir Elton John, spokesperson for an American milk
advertising campaign. Tailor Richard James
Courtesy Richard James Archive

H.M. King Umberto I of Italy conferred his Royal
Warrant on Henry Poole & Co. in 1878
© Private collection/Photo12

An example of the modernization of court dress enacted
by Henry Poole in 1869 in accordance with a request
from Queen Victoria
Courtesy Henry Poole & Co. Archive

The Prince Regent, later King George IV, wearing the
robes of a Knight of the Garter in a portrait by Sir
Thomas Lawrence. Tailor Ede & Ravenscroft
From Una Campbell, *Robes of the Realm: 300 Years of
Ceremonial Dress*. London: Ede & Ravenscroft Ltd., 1989

The seventeenth Duke of Norfolk in full ceremonial dress
as the Earl Marshall. Tailor Ede & Ravenscroft
From Una Campbell, *Robes of the Realm: 300 Years of
Ceremonial Dress*. London: Ede & Ravenscroft Ltd., 1989

Back to formality, London, April 1950
From Martin Harrison, ed., *Parkinson: Photographs
1935–1990*. London: Conran Octopus, 1994

Jack Nicholson as the Joker in *Batman*, USA/UK, 1989,
director Tim Burton. This suit was one of the last projects
overseen by Tommy Nutter prior to his death in 1992
© SNAP Photo Library/GraziaNeri

The Prince of Wales, future King Edward VIII, with his
brother Prince George, Duke of Kent, during a 1927 trip
to America
From Christopher Breward, Edwina Ehrman, Caroline
Evans, *The London Look: Fashion from Street to Catwalk*.
London: Yale University Press, 2004, in collaboration
with the Museum of London

King George V and Queen Mary with the Prince of
Wales, the Duke of Kent, the Princess Royal and the
Duke of Connaught in the annual Royal Ascot race
meeting in 1934. For the King and the Duke, tailor
Davies & Son; for the Prince of Wales, Scholte
From Alfred Cope, ed., *Cope's Royal Cavalcade of the
Turf*. London: Cope's Publication Ltd., 1953

Clarke Gable, a faithful client of Davies & Son
From Marion Maneker, *Dressing in the Dark: Lessons in
Men's Style from the Movies*. New York: Assouline, 2002
Courtesy Photofest

Lily Langtry, Victorian actress and mistress of the Prince
of Wales and future King Edward VII. Tailor Henry
Poole & Co.
Courtesy Henry Poole & Co. Archive

Fred Astaire, 1936. Tailor Anderson & Sheppard
From G. Bruce Boyer, *Fred Astaire Style*. New York:
Assouline, 2004. Courtesy Photofest

Jonathan Ross. Tailor Ozwald Boateng
Page from "Men of the Year," photo Simon Emmett,
GQ UK, no. 208, October 2006

Jonathan Ross add
doggy style to radio'
intergalactic zoo chi

PALE PINK PINSTRIPE
SUIT BY **OZWAL**
BOATENG, £79
020-7437 0620. WHIT
SHIRT BY **WILLIA**
HUNT, £95. 020-743
1921. WHITE BROGUES
£150. CUFF LINKS
MADE TO ORDER
BOTH BY **PAUL SMITH**
020-7379 713
GLASSES, GLOVE
AND PUG, JONATHA
ROSS' OWI

★ RADIO PERSONALIT

Douglas Fairbanks Jr., 1947, before a portrait of his
father Douglas Fairbanks. Tailor Huntsman
© Sipa Press/Olycom

Noel Coward, 1936. Tailor Anderson & Sheppard
From Martin Harrison, ed., *Parkinson: Photographs
1935–1990*. London: Conran Octopus, 1994

Humphrey Bogart. Tailor Hunstman
From Marion Maneker, *Dressing in the Dark: Lessons in
Men's Style from the Movies*. New York: Assouline, 2002
Courtesy Corbis

H.M. Queen Elisabeth II in her coronation robes,
London, June 2, 1953. Tailor Ede & Ravenscroft
From *Robes of the Realm: 300 Years of Ceremonial
Dress*. London: Ede & Ravenscroft Ltd., 1989

THE GREAT BESPOKE
ACCESSORY HOUSES

BERRY BROS. & RUDD

HISTORY

Though it may seem eccentric to include wine and spirit merchant Berry Bros. & Rudd in a consideration of London's finest bespoke accessory houses, it would be a gross omission not to mention this fine firm. Every gentleman who filled his wardrobe at Savile Row probably filled his cellars with fine wines purchased at Berry Bros. & Rudd. The firm is Britain's oldest wine merchant and has traded from the same "old curiosity shop" for over 300 years. Established in 1698 by the widow Bourne at no. 3 St. James's Street, Berry Bros. & Rudd is one of a handful of London shops to retain an eighteenth century shop front largely untouched since the widow's era. The shop is august with its heavily bowed floorboards and colossal weighing scales upon which it was the fashion for grandees from the Regency era through the present day to record their weight. Berry Bros. has a priceless collection of ledgers recording the weights of the great and the good such as the Prince Regent and Lord Byron. Maybe the most historically intriguing record is that of Beau Brummell, one-time friend of the Prince Regent and fashion leader, who was believed to have never returned to London after fleeing his debtors in 1816. Berry Bros. & Rudd possesses the only evidence of the Beau's brief return six years later.

The vaulted cellars beneath Berry Bros. & Rudd are cavernous and include one of the most prestigious private dining rooms in London. Rumor has it that a rabbit warren of tunnels beneath nearby St. James's Palace lead to the vintner's cellars. Did fleeing monarchs Charles II and his brother James II escape England via Berry Bros. & Rudd? Quite possibly. Those lucky enough to visit the parlor on the ground floor of the shop (where partners in years past dined) will see a wall of *Vanity Fair* cartoons of men of consequence including King George V and his son Edward, Prince of Wales. All of the men caricatured are Berry Bros. & Rudd customers, and all are signed.

THE COMPANY TODAY

Berry Bros. & Rudd is still owned and managed by descendants of the Berry and Rudd families. While the shop remains positively Dickensian, the business continues to prosper thanks to early adoption of Internet sales in 1994. The company now has offices in Dublin and Hong Kong as well as two wine schools and the aforementioned private dining room. The pleasure of buying wine from a firm that has already celebrated its tercentenary is its absolute lack of pretension. You may order a modest bottle of Argentinean Malbec as a thank-you for your tailor (as I do) or fill your cellar with cases of Chateau Petrus. The service will be the same.

ROYAL WARRANTS

H.M. the Queen. H.R.H. the Prince of Wales.

FAMOUS/INFAMOUS CUSTOMERS

King George III, the Prince Regent (later George VI), Lord Byron, Prime Minister William Pitt, George "Beau" Brummell, King William IV, Queen Victoria, King Edward VII, King George V, Aga Khan, the Duke of Windsor, King George VI.

ADDRESS

BERRY BROS. & RUDD, 3 St. James's Street, London SW1A 1EG. Tel. +44 207 396 9600. www.bbr.com

GEO F. TRUMPER

HISTORY

George Trumper opened his Mayfair barber's shop on Curzon Street in 1875 conveniently equidistant from Victorian London's great Ducal palaces gathered around Mayfair, St. James's and Park Lane and the court at Buckingham Palace. While working class men paid their penny barber, servants shaved aristocrats in their dressing room. Trumper broke this convention and made it fashionable for men to attend their barber's shop. Trumper made the morning shaving ritual a social occasion. As court hairdresser, Trumper was awarded Queen Victoria's Royal Warrant and his shop became a destination as essential to a man of quality as a club on St. James's Street. Upon the founder's retirement, the legendary George Trumper's feisty daughter headed the company, but she left no heirs so Geo F. Trumper was bought by upwardly mobile West End barber Ivan Bersch.

THE COMPANY TODAY

Ivan Bersch's daughter Paulette now heads the family firm. The shop interiors have changed little since George Trumper's day. The Curzon Street shop is next door to the famous Curzon Street Bookshop where author Nancy Mitford worked, while the Jermyn Street shop keeps the reputation of this prestigious street in the upper echelons of cultivated men's style. Each gentleman is attended to in his own private cubicle should he wish for a shave, haircut, massage or manicure. The shops offer a shaving school service where chaps can be tutored in the fine art of wet shaving and introduced to the glories of Trumper shaving creams, skin foods and colognes.

HOUSE STYLE

Trumper's products have become the gold standard of men's shaving. Many of the house products are named for illustrious customers. The shaving brushes are made from badger hair, the Warwick razors are symphonies in ebony, tortoise shell, faux ivory and gold while the shaving soaps are presented in hand-turned wooden bowls. Trumper's colognes are iconic: Sandalwood, West Indian Lime, Lavender Water, Spanish Leather and Bay Rum. Trumper's Rose, Violet, Coconut Oil, Almond or Lime shaving creams are sublime.

FAMOUS/INFAMOUS CUSTOMERS

The Duke of Wellington, the Duke of Marlborough, Lord Astor, Tom Ford.

ADDRESS

Geo F. Trumper, 9 Curzon Street, London W1J 5HQ. Tel. +44 207 499 1850; 20 Jermyn Street, London SW1Y 6HP. Tel. +44 207 734 1370. www.trumpers.com

G.J. CLEVERLEY & CO.

HISTORY

"Shoemaker of distinction" George Cleverley was born in 1898 to found a shoemaking dynasty. As a child he sold shoelaces and polish, and during World War I he was posted to Calais to toil in a boot factory. He joined Mayfair high society shoemaker Tuczek on Clifford Street and worked for the firm for thirty-eight years before opening his eponymous firm G. J. Cleverley at 27 Cork Street in Mayfair in 1958.

Thus the Cleverley was born: a graceful, chiseled toe shoe that gentlemen from film, finance and high society adopted as a sign of class and quality. George Cleverley ostensibly retired in 1976 and moved the business in with Henry Maxwell on Savile Row. He anointed his successors John Carnera and George Glasgow as the keepers of his flame and continued to work until his death in 1991 when the name passed to the duo, who are now co-owners of Cleverley.

THE COMPANY TODAY

George Glasgow and John Carnera continue to practice the craft of bespoke shoemaking from their shop in the Royal Arcade off Bond Street. Cleverley is without doubt Savile Row's favored shoemaker. Customers are advised to visit Cleverley should they desire shoes as unique as the suits that will accompany them. The shop is tiny: a music box of a space with workrooms upstairs where courtesans once plied their trade.

HOUSE STYLE

Cleverley shoes are as precise, slim and elegant as their iconic customer Fred Astaire.

FAMOUS/INFAMOUS CUSTOMERS

Rudolph Valentino, Sir Winston Churchill, Sir Laurence Olivier, Fred Astaire, Gary Cooper, Sir John Gielgud, Sir Ralph Richardson, Paul Schofield, Humphrey Bogart, Clark Gable, Charles Laughton, Robert Morley, Gloria Swanson, Rex Harrison, the Duke of Bedford, Edward G. Robinson, Jackie Stewart, Terence Stamp, Twiggy, Lennox Lewis, Charlie Watts, Bryan Ferry.

ADDRESS

G.J. CLEVERLEY & CO. LTD., 13 The Royal Arcade, 28 Old Bond Street, London W1S 4SL. Tel. +44 207 493 0443. www.gjcleverley.co.uk

HILDITCH & KEY

HISTORY

Hilditch & Key opened its doors in the final year of the nineteenth century. Founders Charles F. Hilditch and W. Graham Key opened their first shop at the corner of Duke Street and Jermyn Street. The business prospered sufficiently for Hilditch & Key to open an embassy for their shirt making style in Paris on the Rue de Rivoli in 1925. Unlike many of the Savile Row tailors who opened and closed shops in Paris between World War I and World War II, Hilditch & Key endured and remains an elegant outpost of English style in the French capital. Before World War II, Jermyn Street was almost exclusively a shirt maker's street and there was no such thing as a ready-to-wear shirt.

The London shop, meanwhile, was badly bombed during the Blitz, and it was only in 1958 that Hilditch & Key settled at no. 73 Jermyn Street, where they remain today. Hilditch & Key now trades as "makers of the finest quality shirts." In 1978 the company opened a second shop on Jermyn Street at no. 37, as well as a Sloane Street outpost in 1996. In 1981, for the first time in the company's history, Hilditch & Key allowed shops other than their own to sell their shirts.

THE COMPANY TODAY

Under the direction of MD Mr. Michael Booth, Hilditch & Key is pragmatic about its bespoke trade. Booth firmly believes that his off-the-shelf shirts are comparable to the quality of bespoke. "Now all of our shirts are stitched with a single needle and there's less incentive for people to buy bespoke shirts when the quality of off-the-peg is identical," says Booth. "The cut and the choice, of course, remain the only reasons men still order our bespoke shirts." He sees the bespoke as a constant rather than a growing part of the Hilditch & Key business. Booth says, "If you want a bespoke or an off-the-peg shirt, you will not find a better one than Hilditch & Key. You can wear our shirts inside out." Despite the fact that 95% of Hilditch customers are men, Hilditch & Key has a history of making exquisite bespoke shirts for women. But the most prolific bespoke customer is Chanel creative director Karl Lagerfeld, who orders the most extravagant Hilditch & Key shirts with high, Regency collars to compliment his Dior Homme skinny suits.

HOUSE STYLE

A defining characteristic of Hilditch & Key bespoke or off-the-peg shirts is very quiet confidence, not jazzy patterns or extreme details. If Hilditch produces a stripe it hits the mark at every seam. The bestselling shirt is still white or in variations of blue, but Mr. Booth is quite correct that his off-the-peg is sufficiently sublime to question whether bespoke can be any better.

FAMOUS/INFAMOUS CUSTOMERS

P. G. Wodehouse, the Duke of Windsor, Marlene Dietrich, Yves Saint-Laurent, Karl Lagerfeld, Elle Macpherson, Claudia Schiffer, Paloma Picasso, Hedi Slimane.

ADDRESS

HILDITCH & KEY, 73 Jermyn Street, St. James's, London SW1Y 6NP. Tel. +44 207 930 5336. www.hilditchandkey.co.uk

JAMES LOCK & CO.

HISTORY

Founded in 1676, Lock & Co. celebrated its three hundred and thirtieth anniversary in 2006. But the business didn't owe its origins to the Lock family. A Mr. Robert Davies opened his first shop in London. The plague and the great fire of London in 1666 drove the business towards St. James's, next door to the Tudor palace of St. James's and sufficiently close to King Charles the Second's Court at Whitehall. James Lock was an apprentice hired by Robert Davies' son Charles. Lock married the boss's daughter and inherited the business in 1759, changing its name to Lock & Co. Lock moved the firm to no. 6 St. James's Street in 1765 where it remains to this day. The eighteenth century saw the rise of the silk top hat, an accessory Lock came to specialize in. Though Lock's records of 1808 state that George "Beau" Brummell ordered two round hats to be delivered to his Turkish bath (the New Hummuns), it is more than likely that Lock also devised his silk toppers made in a variety of brightly hued silks as opposed to the surviving black antique silk top hats still reconditioned by the house today.

The parish of St. James's is remarkable in that many of the businesses established there in the eighteenth century still trade today, including the booksellers Hatchard's, the vintner Berry Bros. & Rudd, the auctioneer Christie's and the grocer's shop Fortnum & Mason. The secret of these shops' survival, particularly in the case of James Lock, was to "make each customer feel important, as though he were the only customer for whom the whole establishment existed." Mr. Lock also flouted the law, opening the shop on Sundays as he did when Lord Byron came to call from his lodgings a few doors up the street.

It was Lock who made Admiral Lord Nelson's dress uniform hat in 1805, specially-designed with a green silk eyeshade to cover his right eye, which had been blinded in 1794 while the Admiral was at sea. Settling his bill for his "usual" cocked hat and cockade at Lock was one of Nelson's last acts in London before embarking to fight the Battle of Trafalgar.

In 1806 James Lock II succeeded his father. Lock Jr. had delusions of grandeur, ordering a grand equipage when his father rode a horse, and acting the gentleman while his father's estate and earnings were exhausted. Mr. Robert Lincoln eventually bought Lock stock in 1810 while Lock retrenched on his millionaire accoutrements. The third generation, in the persons of James and George Lock, salvaged what was left of the business and brought it back into family hands in 1826. Twelve years later, a young Queen Victoria ascended the throne and signaled the end of the dissolute, degenerate monarchs who had preceded her.

The silk plush tall top hat—with the sheen of a vinyl record—was a totem of Victorian responsibility. Lock was the maestro at making them. Indeed, Lock can be credited with the invention of what we now know as the bowler hat in 1850. The bowler was commissioned by William Coke (a relative of the current Earl of Leicester) to be worn by his gamekeepers as protection against falling pheasants and poachers' sticks. Hence the bowler is still called the "coke at Lock." The trilby, so named for the romantic headgear worn by the mesmeric Svengali in George du Maurier's Victorian novel *Trilby*, was adapted at the end of the nineteenth century from the round hat ordered by Brummell.

The origins for these and other iconic hat shapes are found in Lock's archive. The boater's most famous origin was at Harrow school where the brim was traditionally wider. The fez was a hybrid of the bowler worn by the private detectives who accompanied King Amanullah of Afghanistan on a visit to London in the thirties. The King ordered a gross to take home but Muslim prayers demand that supplicants must touch their foreheads to the ground at prayer. Hence the brims of the cokes were snipped off. Come the revolution the orders Lock expected to flood in never did.

George Lock died in 1865. Charles Whitbourn, his gentrified nephew, was enticed into the family firm by uncle James. In 1871 uncle James passed the business to Charles and Mr. James Benning. The name survived, but royal patronage was briefly withheld when Lock refused to extend credit to the Prince of Wales's "friends" as sweeteners to the future King Edward VII's own debts. Edward VII boycotted Lock, as did his son George V. However, the rebellious trendsetting Edward, Prince of Wales (later Duke of Windsor) took great delight in flouting his father and grandfather and became a lifelong customer of Lock.

The Duke of Windsor was not dissimilar to George Clooney today. What he wore became the mirror of fashion. From Lock he ordered silk top hats, cokes, trilbys, straw hats and tweed flat caps that he wore to play golf. It was a Lock straw hat that he wore trimmed with a black satin band when his father died, thus shocking the establishment. Queen Mary, Edward's mother, wrote to Lock insisting that her son was not extended credit. There was no need for maternal caution. The Prince paid his bills as far as his sartorial servants were concerned.

Lock & Co. has served the royal family ever since, advising the Duke of Edinburgh how to acclimatize himself to his annual appearance in his Guards' bearskin, and aiding Garrard & Co. remodel the Imperial State Crown for the new Queen Elizabeth II in 1953 to devise a modern fitment that would sit lightly on the monarch's head. The 1971 book *Mr. Lock of St. James's Street* records the Queen being fitted for the Imperial State Crown at Buckingham Palace by Mr. Lock and declaring "Isn't it funny—it fits."

THE COMPANY TODAY

Lock & Co. is the oldest family-owned and run hat shop in the world. Chairman Nigel Lock MacDonald is a direct descendant of the founder James Lock. The shop retains Elizabethan details in its architectural frame and remains in family hands. Along with John Lobb and Berry Bros. & Rudd, it is one of the most unspoiled commercial premises in London. Visiting Lock is a constant delight. You may find yourself next to an aristocratic member of White's Club ordering the selfsame homburg he orders once a decade. You may be consorting with a black hip hop artist who is beguiled by the trilby. The firm is as likely to be loaning hats for a *Dazed & Confused* fashion shoot as it is to be selling a reconditioned Edwardian black silk plush top hat to a Rothschild or Goldsmith to sport at Royal Ascot. Anything is possible at Lock, from a yachting cap in the style of George V to a fez, an astrakhan hat made for a former President of Afghanistan, a chauffeur's peaked cap complete with livery, or an immaculate coke. The history and the future in the making is the pride of this ancient firm.

HOUSE STYLE

The house style is the history of bespoke hat making.

ROYAL WARRANTS

H.R.H. the Duke of Edinburgh, H.R.H. the Prince of Wales.

FAMOUS/INFAMOUS CUSTOMERS

Admiral Lord Nelson, the Duke of Wellington, Lord Byron, George "Beau" Brummell, Pitt the Younger, Horace Walpole, the Prince Regent (later King George VI), the 3rd Earl of March (Old Q), David Garrick, John Nash, Oscar Wilde, Lewis Carroll, Cecil Beaton, the Duke of Marlborough, the Duke of Bedford, the Duke of Windsor, Evelyn Waugh, Sir Winston Churchill, Charlie Chaplin, Douglas Fairbanks Jr., Frank Sinatra, Sir Alec Guinness, Sir Laurence Olivier, Charles Laughton, Salvador Dalí, Harold Macmillan, Graham Greene, Jackie Kennedy, Bryan Ferry, Madonna, Guy Ritchie, Johnny Depp.

ADDRESS

JAMES LOCK & CO., 6 St. James's Street, London SW1A 1EF. Tel. +44 207 930 8874.
www.lockhatters.co.uk

JOHN LOBB

HISTORY

John Lobb Ltd. has the distinction of residing in the same building as "mad, bad and dangerous to know" Lord Byron's bachelor quarters. The shop is in the shadow of London's finest Tudor Palace (St. James's Palace) and is surrounded by eminent gentlemen's clubs and purveyors of gentlemen's requisites as old as London aristocratic society itself.

The firm's founder, John Lobb, was rather uncharitably described as "a lame Cornish farm boy who mastered the gentle craft of last and awl" in Lobb's 1972 biography *The Last Shall be First*. Mr. Lobb went on to win the Royal Warrant of Edward, Prince of Wales (later King Edward VII) in 1863. But it wasn't a smooth transition from farm boy to shoemaker for the Edwardian glitterati. At 20, John Lobb went up to London and floundered. Trying his luck in Australia in

1832, John Lobb made sufficient money making shoes for the burgeoning community of gold mining prospectors to return to London and open his first eponymous shop at 296 Regent Street. Lobb's tenure in Australia prompted the witticism "There's gold in them thar heels" (a variation of which Alfred Hitchcock used to compliment Grace Kelly in a metallic Edith Head gown when he declared "There's hills in them thar gold"). John Lobb's reputation grew until he became the preeminent bespoke boot maker in London. Unfortunately—as is so lamentably often the case in family firms—his sons were less than worthy inheritors of his legacy. John Lobb Jr., who had scandalized his upwardly mobile father by marrying a chorus girl, was caught with his hand in the till and dismissed. When Lobb Sr. died in 1895, he made a deathbed amendment and his son was cut off without a penny. John Lobb's younger son, William, inherited the eponymous firm and, on the death of the King, his son George V remained as loyal to William Lobb as his father was to John.

In 1901, William Hunter Lobb had expanded the business and opened a branch in Paris, as well as expanding his London empire to St. James's Street. After William Hunter Lobb's premature death in 1916, his widow Betsy steered the firm in absentia through the First World War by employing the autocratic Moore family as caretakers of John Lobb. Her three sons weren't of an age or possessing sufficient experience to step into their father's boots. Thus by the thirties, John Lobb teetered on the brink of bankruptcy. Once again, the younger son (Eric Lobb) saved the family firm.

A combination of Eric's colorblindness (which disqualified him from entering the forces in 1939 when World War II was declared), and the British government decreeing it essential that Lobb remain trading to contribute to the war effort locked Eric Lobb into the managing director's chair for life. Eric cleverly evacuated all of the ledgers and lasts from the St. James's shop and thus saved the firm's history. It was he who encouraged the firm to treat six German bombs hitting successive shops on St. James's Street during the Blitz as little more than tiresome interruptions. Eric brought the Royal Warrant back to the firm—first the Duke of Edinburgh's in 1956 and then H.M. the Queen's in 1963.

John Lobb continued to create bespoke shoes and boots for kings, prime ministers, maharajahs, eminent authors and men of fashion throughout its turbulent history. The firm's archives record such colorful customers as Oscar Wilde's feckless poet acolyte Lord Alfred Douglas (or "Bosie," as Wilde christened him). American idols such as publishing giant Condé Nast, jazz age author F. Scott Fitzgerald and composer Cole Porter patronized the firm in the twenties. Hollywood followed in the shape of Katharine Hepburn, Laurence Olivier, Tyrone Power and Fred Astaire. Socialites such as the Duke of Windsor, Duff Cooper and Cecil Beaton set fashions with their Lobb bespoke shoes.

Mr. Eric Lobb was still going strong in the seventies, when the firm commissioned Brian Dobbs to write The Last Shall be First. Like many of the Savile Row tailors, he had heeded the Post-War call to America in the fifties and successfully exported great British bespoke while the home market floundered. This glittering reputation as an international business that John Lobb maintained as the twentieth century came to a close attracted the acquisitive eye of French luxury goods house Hermès. Hermès acquired the name John Lobb to trade under it worldwide for ready-made and made-to-measure shoes. And yet no. 9 St. James's Street—John Lobb's final home—remains in the family's hands and continues to trade as the original London bespoke shoe business from that single shop.

THE COMPANY TODAY

John Hunter Lobb, a direct descendant of John Lobb, is the guardian of the company's illustrious flame. He sits in a first floor office surrounded by signed checks from some of the firm's most illustrious customers. By his side is a book filled with the outlines of famous feet that the house has shod. Esquire described no. 9 as "the most beautiful shop in the world" and with some justification. The shop front is flanked by the bespoke workshop and is a living museum of bespoke shoemaking. Glass cases bear testament to the firm's heritage as shoemaker to the giants of twentieth century history. Lobb can match Savile Row name for illustrious name from its extensive ledgers.

Beneath the shop floor is a cavernous basement holding thousands of wooden lasts held by the firm for existing customers, plus a library full of ledgers and a small cupboard containing lasts of late customers. The most poignant is the late Diana, Princess of Wales's last. The firm made shoes for her as Lady Diana Spencer. This was crossed out when she became H.R.H the Princess of Wales and was crossed out again when she lost the H.R.H and became simply Diana, Princess of Wales until her death in 1997.

John Lobb Ltd. is a survivor. The name continues to execute the craft of bespoke shoe and boot making with a superb indifference to the dumbing-down of production in the twenty-first century. This dedication to upholding standards and celebrating hand craftsmanship is the strength of John Lobb Ltd.

HOUSE STYLE
Lobb is a master in crafting any bespoke shoe you may desire, be that a patent leather evening slipper with *grosgrain* bow, a jazzy pair of black and white two-tone brogues, the definitive black cap-toed Oxford or the most superb pair of riding boots. Nothing is beyond John Lobb's bespoke capabilities.

ROYAL WARRANTS
H.M. the Queen (boot makers), H.R.H. the Duke of Edinburgh (boot makers), H.R.H. the Prince of Wales (boot makers).

FAMOUS/INFAMOUS CUSTOMERS
King Edward VII, Enrico Caruso, Lord Alfred Douglas (or Bosie, Oscar Wilde's lover), Frank Harris (king of pornography), George Bernard Shaw, John Galsworthy, the Maharajah of Cooch Behar, Prince Louis Esterhazy, Condé Nast, Cole Porter, Ronald Firbank, Jonathan Cape, Katharine Hepburn, the Shah of Iran, the Emperor of Ethiopia, the King of Thailand, Bernard "DeBeers" Oppenheimer, the Maharajah of Baroda, Vernon Castle, Norman Hartnell, Duff Cooper, Hugh Walpole, Somerset Maugham, Leslie Charteris, the Maharajah of Jaipur, Douglas Jardine, Amy Johnson, Cecil Beaton, George Balanchine, Leonide Massine, Randolph Churchill, Sir Hardy Amies, the Duke of Windsor, Jack Buchanan, Sir Laurence Olivier, Orson Welles, Frank Sinatra, Gregory Peck, Laurence Harvey, Anthony Blunt, Joseph Pulitzer, Prime Ministers Neville Chamberlain and Harold Macmillan, Peter O'Toole, the Duke of Bedford, King Hussein of Jordan, Diana Princess of Wales, Roald Dahl, Charles Clore, Sir David Frost, Mick Jagger, Twiggy.

ADDRESS
JOHN LOBB LTD., 9 St. James's Street, London SW1A 1EF. Tel. +44 207 930 3664. www.johnlobbltd.co.uk

SWAINE ADENEY BRIGG

HISTORY

Founded in 1750, the company specializes in equestrian and country clothing and has grown to include bespoke leather goods and umbrellas. The founding father was John Ross who opened his whip making shop at no. 238 Piccadilly. James Swaine bought Ross out in 1798 having worked for a rival whip maker in Holborn. Swaine Adeney soon acquired the Royal Warrant for King George VIII as well as the Prince Regent and the Dukes of York, Clarence, Kent, Cumberland and Cambridge. James Swaine moved the business to 185 Piccadilly in 1835, having retained the Royal Warrant of King George VI and King William IV, invited his nephew into the firm and christened it Swaine Adeney. Swaine Adeney was one of the Victorian companies to display their craft at the Crystal Palace during the 1851 Great Exhibition. The company then went on to show at the 1900 Paris Exhibition.

Meanwhile, umbrella specialist Thomas Brigg was established in 1836 at 23 St. James's Street, capitalizing on the fashion for fops and dandies of toting umbrellas, sticks and hunting crops in society and attending the daily social gathering on Rotten Row. In 1893, Queen Victoria awarded Thomas Brigg her Royal Warrant, an honor the firm enjoys to this day. In 1943, after having lost its Paris shop during the Nazi occupation, Brigg allied with Swaine Adeney. Brigg gained international notoriety when it created a Malacca-handled umbrella for the character of Steed in the sixties TV show *The Avengers* that concealed first a blade and then a gun. It was the Brigg umbrella that the KGB doctored so that its spies in London could inject a lethal dose of Rican into their victims' bloodstreams. Thus Swaine Adeney Brigg & Sons Ltd. has become an icon of lethal gentleman's style. The Prince of Wales has Brigg umbrellas specially made with detachable handle and tip so he can travel with an immaculate British made umbrella to the former empire and colonies worldwide.

THE COMPANY TODAY

Swaine Adeney Brigg now trades from a grand shop front on St. James's Street. The business prides itself on bespoke but sells English gentlemen's requisites off-the-peg. The shop interior is new and may need one hundred years to settle into its new home. Nevertheless, all of Swaine Adeney's leather is still produced in their Cambridgeshire workshops and made from hides reared in the UK. As a consequence, Swaine Adeney Brigg's bride leather is the finest in the world. Herbert Johnson, the hatter incorporated into Swaine Adeney Brigg, enjoyed a fashion moment in the eighties when visited by Stephen Spielberg and Harrison Ford who wanted an iconic hat for their fictional hero Indiana Jones. Johnson suggested a tall crowned, wide brim fur felt hat called "the poet" that had been made since the end of the nineteenth century. The firm pulled the brim down to give "an explorer/safari look," thereby creating the most desirable hat of the decade.

ROYAL WARRANTS

H.M. the Queen (whip and glove makers), H.M. Queen Elizabeth the Queen Mother (umbrella makers), H.R.H. the Prince of Wales (suppliers of umbrellas).

ADDRESS

SWAINE ADENEY BRIGG LTD., 54 St. James's Street, London SW1A 1JT. Tel. +44 207 409 7277. www.swaineadeney.co.uk

TURNBULL & ASSER

HISTORY

1885 saw the opening of John Arthur Turnbull at no. 3 Church Place, a small alleyway facing St. James's Church Piccadilly (where Beau Brummell's grandparents are buried). The tiny alley joined Jermyn Street and Piccadilly, two essential streets for the gentleman of quality in the late nineteenth century. The hosier and glove maker was co-founded by Reginald Turnbull and Ernest Asser. In the grand tradition of Savile Row, the former was a craftsman and the latter a great salesman. This combination of skill and public relations rarely fails.

By 1895 Ernest Asser had talked his way into acknowledgement above the shop front alongside Turnbull's. Trade was brisk in the broadest collection of gentlemen's requisites: shirts, undergarments, dressing gowns, smoking jackets, braces, ties and pocket silks. In 1903, Turnbull, Asser & Co. outgrew its premises and opened an emporium and workrooms that spanned the corners of Jermyn Street and Bury Street below a grand set of bachelor quarters then called Marlborough House (rather presumptuously after the Prince of Wales's London residence on the Mall). The firm remains at nos. 71 and 72 Jermyn Street to this day.

Opening a shop beneath this rabbit warren of wealthy single men was as effective for Messrs. Turnbull & Asser as it was for the many houses of ill repute that traditionally crowded this gentlemen's quarter of London. But the aforementioned Prince of Wales's reign as King Edward VII was the sunset of the British Empire and ended with the death of the King and the declaration of World War I in 1914. Turnbull & Asser's proficiency in sporting and outdoor requisites equipped the firm well for the Great War.

Coats, raincoats and "The Oilskin Combination Coverall & Ground Sheet" were sold to promote morale and protect British soldiers and civilians. Its concentration on the burgeoning women's trade earned the company its first Royal Warrant under the patronage of H.M. Queen Alexandra.

The twenties brought jazz, booze and glamour back to London. With it came a new leader of fashion in the shape of the dashing Edward, Prince of Wales. A keen steeplechaser, golfer and tennis player, the Prince flouted the formal, Edwardian dress codes upheld by his father King George V. Turnbull & Asser realigned their business as shirt specialists and made sublime, dynamic sport-led shirts in crepe-de-chine, cashmere and poplins. Modeled by the Prince of Wales, Turnbull & Asser's jazz age shirting dazzled London society. During this era, Turnbull & Asser customer F. Scott Fitzgerald wrote his iconic novel, *The Great Gatsby*, in which he reduced his socialite heroine Daisy to tears at the beauty of Gatsby's imported shirts. When Robert Redford starred in the eponymous 1973 film, his emotionally charged shirts are clearly bought at Turnbull & Asser.

The firm dressed the man of the hour during World War II, Prime Minister Churchill, who was oft photographed wearing one of Turnbull & Asser's zip-front, belted "romper suits."

The coronation of Queen Elizabeth II in 1953 and a Hollywood golden age in "glorious Technicolor" brought the firm a boom time when the new court revived the craft of formal Edwardian evening and ceremonial shirts while Hollywood royalty Cary Grant, David Niven and Frank Sinatra led fashion in bespoke Turnbull & Asser shirts.

In 1963, Turnbull & Asser was responsible for launching one of the most swinging men's wear designers of the era onto London. Michael Fish was a rather exotic sales assistant who created the fat, wide tie christened "the kipper." Fish would go on to open his own boutique on Clifford Street, but Turnbull & Asser had the distinction of being the birthplace of the sixties "supersize-me" ties and bow ties. The firm has made all of James Bond's shirts from his first screen outing in 1962 (Sean Connery) to the present (Daniel Craig). A double-cuff evening shirt buttoned with pearls was an early innovation that Turnbull & Asser continues to make today. Prince Charles remains one of the firm's most iconic customers. In 1981 his mother allowed Prince Charles to confer the Royal Warrant and Turnbull & Asser was the first company he chose. When the Prince broke his arm in 1990, Turnbull & Asser created bespoke one-armed shirts and slings for the Prince of Wales. The Prince has since chosen Turnbull & Asser to create made-to-measure suits for him in addition to his shirts and ties.

Turnbull & Asser was a rare taste shared between the Prince and Princess of Wales. In one of the most heartfelt tributes to the late Diana, Princess of Wales, Turnbull & Asser went on record as saying "the company was completely devastated by the news of her tragic death on August 31, 1997. A wonderful person has been lost, a good friend and a kind and considerate customer who always lit up the whole shop with her star-bright quality when she called at Jermyn Street. A Diana-day was always a very happy day for the staff." In 1997, the firm added an East 57th Street flagship (at the corner of 42nd Street in New York City) to its established presence at Bergdorf Goodman.

THE COMPANY TODAY
Turnbull & Asser truly has one of the most magnificent shops in London. One is aware that this is a house founded in the Edwardian age of elegance, and very clever lighting casts a warm, golden glow over gentlemen's requisites that at first glance have not changed since the turn of the twentieth century. But look closer. The shop is a library of gentleman's accessories and can accommodate both the nostalgic and the modern customer. You want a feather-light smoking jacket? The house will make one for you. You want silk socks that don't disintegrate after one white tie ball? The house has the hosiery for you. Everything is possible, from stiff Ascot collars to woven silk ties of just the correct weight.

In 1971, Turnbull & Asser perceptively opened the Churchill Room doors away from its flagship corner. This shop is dedicated to the fine art of handmade shirts and contains every shirting and tie cloth imaginable under the sun. This is where the house's bespoke customers order their shirts. *Turnbull & Asser*, a history penned by Nicholas Foulkes in 1997, records that "the largest single (bespoke) order ever recorded was by the Sultan of Oman who ordered 240 shirts in twenty minutes."

The Sultan may be the firm's most prolific customer, but he is not the most inventive. Artist Sebastian Horsley has developed a silk gauntlet cuff with a regiment of covered silk buttons. In the seventies, head of Paramount Pictures Robert Evans developed a collar that impressed Sammy Davis Jr. sufficiently for him to order fifty for himself. The house records Picasso's penchant for polka dots and Charlie Chaplin's appetite for silk pajamas, which he ordered in double digits.

The renaissance in bespoke shirt making has made the Churchill Room a destination as glamorous to London's young bucks as Aspinall's, S.J. Phillips or Hamilton's Gallery.

HOUSE STYLE
Nowhere is Turnbull & Asser's finesse between traditional values and the twenty-first century as elegantly demonstrated as worn by Daniel Craig as 007 in *Casino Royale*. Turnbull & Asser accompanies this action man with an athletic figure from morning to night through *soignée* gaming rooms and into Venetian palazzos, where he never once looks out of step or out of place. The house could wish for no more suitable poster boy in 2007.

ROYAL WARRANTS
H.R.H. the Prince of Wales (shirt makers).

FAMOUS/INFAMOUS CUSTOMERS

H.M. Queen Alexandra, Sir Winston Churchill, F. Scott Fitzgerald, the Duke of Windsor, Picasso, Charlie Chaplin, Cary Grant, David Niven, Robert Redford, David Hemmings, Liberace, Brian Epstein, Jean Shrimpton, Sean Connery, Bianca Jagger, Sammy Davis Jr., Roger Moore, Donald Sutherland, Albert Finney, Mel Brooks, Patrick McNee, Al Pacino, President Ronald Reagan, Michael Caine, Sir John Gielgud, Richard Attenborough, Pierce Brosnan, the Sultan of Oman, the late Diana, Princess of Wales, Daniel Craig (as 007), Stephen Fry.

ADDRESS

TURNBULL & ASSER, 71 and 72 Jermyn Street, St. James's, London SW1Y 6PF
Tel. +44 207 808 3000. www.turnbullandasser.com

THE CLOTH HOUSES
AND GREAT BRITISH MILLS

Sportex
by DORMEUIL
REGD.

Scotland's most exclusive cloth

INTRODUCTION

DAVID HARVEY

Weaving in England is one of the oldest recorded occupations outside the church. A tax roll dated 1130 established the official existence of a guild of weavers in the City of London. Guilds and religious foundations based on crafts were a common feature of corporate identity and protection throughout Christian Europe in medieval times. London has happily retained not only many of the magnificent edifices raised by these guilds but also maintained the active professional and social activities performed within them. Today the Worshipful Company of Weavers is one of the longest surviving institutions of its kind. Their contemporary program and educational funding have brought the company firmly into the twenty-first century.

Weaving is integral to the whole tailoring craft and the role of some of the most distinguished British mills and cloth houses in supporting the London Cut is a simple, but serious, illustration of the basic precept of dress: without cloth there can be no suit. Early recorded history of weaving in England is that of the kingdom itself, exemplified by the reign of Edward III in particular who imposed stiff rules about trading in wool and defined qualities of fleece and yarn. The guild's historian, Valerie Hope, points out that wool trade was the bedrock of England and Scotland's medieval economy and (no pun intended) very much the fabric of this country's history. A Tudor cloth merchant in London was of sufficient import to have his wife, Mrs. Nicholas Small, painted by Henry VIII's court painter Hans Holbein in 1540. The portrait was exhibited at Tate Britain's grand Holbein retrospective in October 2006.

As England's trade with Europe grew, so did the need for some kind of holding system—hence the merchant (or "cloth houses" as they prefer to be called). Direct contact between a weaver in London and a local tailor was relatively simple in the early forms of town and country life. But growing populations, distance and local industrial concentrations of particular products (for example Yorkshire as the base of much of the wool processing industry) imposed different solutions to supply and demand. Trading activity between British towns, coupled with the growing dominance of British mercantile trade, had already encouraged a merchant or trading system with a middle man securing the weavers' products and holding them for wider distribution to the tailoring industry both home and overseas.

In Scotland a domestic loom was often a critical means of subsistence for isolated crofters, relying on the clip from their sheep to supply the yarn for rough and ready cloth. This the weaver brought to the nearest town, perhaps being paid in kind while the merchant took over the cloth and often finished it for making up. Intrepid Savile Row guv'nors passionate about Scottish tweed such as Norton & Sons' Patrick Grant roam the Highlands to form personal relationships with these weavers. Kilgour's Carlo Brandelli mines Huddersfield's rich seam of cloth mills in pursuit of exclusivity and excellence. Of course the merchant's bunch (presented in library books of cloth) are a vital component in any Savile Row bespoke tailor's shop. Customers may select suiting from a bunch and yet tailor and customer may well be unaware of the mill that produced that cloth.

The merchant's bunch, by its very nature, is a complex collection of qualities and designs. The Anglo-French merchant house of Dormeuil has virtually all its cloth woven in Yorkshire, while Brussels and Savile Row-based Scabal use several British resources as well as continental weavers. The lion's share of the cloth houses represented in *The London Cut*—Dugdale Brothers & Co., Holland & Sherry and Lear, Brown & Dunsford Ltd.—are British born and bred.

THE GREAT CLOTH HOUSES

DORMEUIL

Uniquely, Dormeuil is an Anglo-French business established in 1842 with both London and Paris branches and specializing in wool and silk cloth. By 1880 Dormeuil had a shop front in New York City. As early as the sixties, the cloth house was producing its own ready-to-wear collection under the direction of Serge Dufor-Dormeuil. Today, under the leadership of Dominique Dormeuil, the family still controls a global business in directly selling the finest cloth to the tailoring and manufacturing sectors. An increasingly vertical operation is bringing immense textile resources to its own successful retail outlets. Today Dormeuil has one of the grandest townhouses on Sackville Street. The house's neighbor on Sackville Street—a street that once rivaled the Row as London's home of bespoke tailoring—is designer Jasper Conran's townhouse. While the company commissions textiles from several countries, the majority of its cloth is woven in Yorkshire. The company has made a significant contribution to contemporary sales methods by audacious advertising, leading the way in the seventies with a dramatic poster campaign which transformed the traditional approach to marketing by aiming at the customer rather than the supplier. Like the great Parisian couture house Yves Saint Laurent and Champs Elysees cabaret club the Lido, Dormeuil commissioned Rene Gruau (arguably one of the greatest twentieth century fashion illustrators) to create iconic advertisements for the house. A classic promotion used the Tonik quality with top sixties model Veruschka (Vera von Lehndorff) wearing chic Savile Row men's suits.

ADDRESS
DORMEUIL, 35 Sackville Street, London W1S 3EG. Tel. +44 207 439 3723. www.dormeuil.com

DUGDALE BROTHERS & CO.

Family tradition still holds for British merchants and Dugdale Brothers & Co. is run by the third generation of the Charnock family, retaining the entity of Fisher & Company, which was established in 1859 as a major exporter of worsted fabrics throughout Europe and America. The company was noted for opening up South America to Yorkshire fabrics. Today Dugdale specializes in crossbred wool and Merino, cavalry twills, superfine worsteds and cashmere suitings and overcoatings.

ADDRESS
DUGDALE BROTHERS & CO. LTD., 5 Northumberland Street, Huddersfield, West Yorkshire. Tel. +44 148 442 1772.

HARRISONS OF EDINBURGH

The story of Harrisons of Edinburgh encompasses the struggles and romance of Scottish textiles. Established in Edinburgh in 1863 by Sir George Harrison (formerly an Edinburgh tailor's apprentice), Harrisons of Edinburgh continued the age-old custom of buying in rough cloth brought into town by solitary weavers. This was often their only means of livelihood. The firm developed a finishing business and played a prominent role in the establishment of "district checks"; a designation for most of the new textile patterns developed for Scottish landowners in the nineteenth century. Harrisons developed the Burns check, sported around the world by Scotsmen on Burns Night, and supplied Great Britain's royal family with the Balmoral check originally designed by Queen Victoria's consort Prince Albert for exclusive use on the Balmoral estate. The company now forms part of the Lear, Brown & Dunsford group.

ADDRESS
HARRISONS OF EDINBURGH, 45 Queen Street, Edinburgh EH2 3NH. Tel. +44 131 220 5775 www.lbd-harrisons.com

HOLLAND & SHERRY

In spite of the assumption that merchants are simply handing cloth on from the mill to the tailor, several companies have large international profiles. In Britain, Scottish-based Holland and Sherry celebrated its 170th anniversary in 2006. The previous chairman, Anthony Holland, was the great grandson of the founder and the company has offices in Australia, France, Hong Kong, the US and Italy. Fabric trade has been the mainstay of the business since the beginning, selling to individual tailors around the world, Parisian couture houses and international retailers. The company has its own weaving and finishing capacity as well as resourcing luxury cloths that are often blended with rare and exotic fibers. A recent development is Shahmina, a cloth competing with cashmere at half the price, with a fifteen-micron count and density of eight to ten thousand hairs per square centimeter. The company's products have featured in many films and, ten years ago, it began to diversify into high quality textiles for interior design.

ADDRESS
HOLLAND & SHERRY, PO Box 1, Venlaw Road, Peebles, Scotland EH45 8RN. Tel. +44 172 172 0101. www.hollandandsherry.com

LEAR, BROWN & DUNSFORD

Originally founded in 1895, Lear, Brown & Dunsford is currently owned by brothers Richard and Peter Dunsford who have maintained the luxury and country cloth specialization that bears their name. The merchant business operates in Britain and internationally, dealing in luxury cashmere jacketing and overcoats, fine quality wools and mohair blends (featuring super 120s, 130s and 150s), Scottish tweeds and country cloths. Various acquisitions have expanded both the company's field of operations and its wide range of qualities to embrace not only classic Scottish types but also materials from competitive suitings and uniforms. The Dunsford brothers' sons, James and Mark, will be the fourth generation of the family to head this eminent cloth house. The Lear, Brown & Dunsford empire now includes Harrisons of Edinburgh, Pedersen & Becker, A.L. Robinson and Porter & Harding.

ADDRESS
LEAR, BROWN & DUNSFORD LTD., LBD House, Waterbridge Court, Matford Park Road, Exeter. www.lbd-harrisons.com

SCABAL

Another major international weaver and merchant business is the Belgian Scabal Group, founded in Brussels in 1938 by Otto Herz. The exotic name is an abbreviation of Société Commerciale Anglo, Belgo, Allemande & Luxembourgeoise and today employs over 600 people around the world. Scabal supplies couture-quality textiles to the top end of the market such as Yangir, a cloth sourced from a Mongolian goat reputed to be softer than cashmere. Scabal is the only cloth house to have a home on Savile Row at no. 12. The group has developed both ready-to-wear and bespoke operations, and launches a bespoke suit christened the "no. 12" at Pitti Uomo in January 2007. Scabal resources its own textiles from a Yorkshire mill and its clothing from a factory in Saabrucken. Each season Scabal identifies a particular fabric range such as their famous pinstripe spun with pure gold, lapis lazuli or diamond dust. "Golden Treasure" was the cloth from which the new James Bond (Daniel Craig's) suits were cut for the 2006 movie *Casino Royale*. Scabal has previously dressed great menswear movies such as *GoldenEye, Casino, The Untouchables, The Godfather III, Titanic* and *The Aviator*. The late surrealist Salvador Dalí executed a collection of drawings inspired by men's clothing that remain in the company's Brussels headquarters. Dalí, who famously collaborated with the French couturier Elsa Schiaparelli, did not consider men's fashion as a subject before or after Scabal's commission. A collection of cloths inspired by the company's prized Dalí collection, entitled a "Tribute to Dalí," was woven by Scabal to mark the artist's centenary.

ADDRESS
SCABAL, no. 12 Savile Row, London W1S 3PQ. Tel. +44 207 734 1867. www.scabal.com

THE GREAT BRITISH CLOTH MILLS

BOWER ROEBUCK & CO.

Waterpower drove the first cloth fulling machines in the Yorkshire valleys, and wool production began on the Bower Roebuck & Co. site in the sixteenth century. The original company was the first to install mechanized wool carding machines in 1779 and the tradition of innovation has been sustained with computerized sampling and high-tech machinery. Messrs. Bower and Roebuck founded the present operation in 1899, building a reputation for weaving the highest quality counts. Within the Scabal group, the mill pioneered a super 120's quality, one micron finer than the then established super 100's. More recently Bower Roebuck & Co. developed super 150's using a 15.3-micron wool. Even now the company is developing even finer yarn counts, producing qualities as light as 165 grams alongside cashmere/silk blends and 100% cashmere suiting.

ADDRESS
BOWER ROEBUCK & CO. LTD., Glendale Mills, New Mill, Huddersfield, West Yorkshire, HD9 7EN. Tel. +44 148 468 2181.

CHARLES CLAYTON

The Bodikian family, which owns Charles Clayton, is in its fourth generation at the helm of the company they bought in 1963. Charles Clayton concentrates on only the finest quality fabrics from the finest raw materials. The product is a range of luxury fabrics made from cashmere, wool, silk and other noble fibers focused largely on men's wear. Charles Clayton is another mill that can claim it uses the softest water drawn from deep wells using natural soaps without any synthetic additives during the washing and finishing process. Uncrushable qualities of cloth and high luster finishes are a specialty of the house.

ADDRESS
CHARLES CLAYTON, Riverside Mills, Salleworth Road, Elland, West Yorkshire HX5 ORY. Tel. +44 142 237 7000. www.charlesclayton.co.uk

EDWIN WOODHOUSE & CO. LTD.

Trading since 1858 but incorporated in 1898, Edwin Woodhouse & Co. is one of the few vertical operations left in Yorkshire: moving the product from wool tops through yarn dyeing to twisting, warping, weaving, piece dyeing and finishing. Specialists in high quality worsted fabrics, the Gaunt family has owned the operation for four generations and easily combines modern electronically controlled equipment alongside more traditional methods to produce the mill's recognizable qualities.

ADDRESS
EDWIN WOODHOUSE & CO. LTD., Sunny Bank Mills, Farsley, Pudsey, West Yorkshire LS28 5UJ. Tel. +44 113 257 4331. www.edwin-woodhouse.co.uk

JOHNSTONS OF ELGIN

Probably the oldest continuously owned weaver in the British Isles, Johnstons of Elgin is based in Morayshire, Northern Scotland, and was founded in 1797. The company has remained in family hands ever since. The mill pioneered cashmere and Vicuna weaving in Scotland in 1851 and today increasingly concentrates on cashmere, weaving apparel cloth and knitting at another unit in Hawick (the Scottish Lowlands). The mill is the only one in Britain that takes cashmere from raw material to the finished article. Historically, Johnstons of Elgin played a crucial part in the benchmark of Scottish fabric design—district checks or "estate tweeds"—devised to identify people who lived and worked in the same area and very often for the same employer or landowner. Many of these designs have been modified and taken into general ranges. The constant variation of these basic patterns continues to inspire the range of luxurious jackets, skirts, shawls and scarves.

ADDRESS
JOHNSTONS OF ELGIN, Newmill, Elgin, Morayshire, Scotland IV30 4AF. Tel. +44 134 355 4000. www.johnstonscashmere.com

LASSIERE MILLS

Founded in 1949, Lassiere Mills Ltd. is a union of French style and English tradition. This family-owned business still produces the finest cloth and specializes in fine yarns with modern finishes. This has secured a foundation for the company's international operations. Fabric yarns range from pure Mongolian worsted cashmere to 100% pure silk-2fold, mohair/wool and all wool luxury lends. Summer suitings weigh from 200 to 260 grams and winter weights run from 260 to 350 grams. Lassiere Mills cloth features in many top Italian suiting brand collections.

ADDRESS

LASSIERE MILLS LTD., Unit 22, Albion Mill, Albion Road, Greengates, West Yorkshire BD10 9TQ. Tel. +44 127 461 3700. www.lassieremills.co.uk

MOXON

Moxon, founded in 1887, specializes in fancy weaves with a determined policy of never repeating a motif or a piece. Exclusivity has been the aim of the Moxon mill through several generations and owners. Coupled with rarity and use of the finest wool and cashmere fibers, the mill is famous for its oft-copied initial pinstripes. The concept was launched with much fanfare as Moxon made a gift of "JC" pinstripe cloth (a repeat graphic of the gentlemen's initials) to both American President James Carter and British Prime Minister James Callaghan. Bespoke (or custom design if you're a US citizen) at this luxury level is an important element in the company's success. Many of its suitings are priced well above similar Italian cloths and Spencer Hart's founder/designer Nick Hart is messianic about Moxon for his black and midnight blue cocktail suiting.

ADDRESS

MOXON, Brigella Mills, Bradford BD5 OQA. Tel. +44 127 452 5500.

REID & TAYLOR

A local weaver named Reid secured financing from a Mr. Taylor, thus founding a world famous textile label on the banks of the river Esk in the Scottish Borders. The original product of heavy cloth made from local Cheviot wools was upturned later in the twentieth century when a new proprietor initiated the then unusual (and highly visual) public relations campaign around the company's logo of a top hatted ram bearing the legend: "The finest Double Twist Worsted in the World." The complex weaves were rich in buried color, inspiring comparisons of the cloth with stained glass or painting techniques. Reid & Taylor fabrics maintain this tradition of intense design in the finest fibers, be they Golden Bale or Blue Ross-shire cheviot.

ADDRESS

REID & TAYLOR, William Street, Langholm, Scotland DG13 OBN. Tel. +44 138 738 03121.

TAYLOR & LODGE

More than 120 years of experience has contributed to the current status of Taylor & Lodge. The firm's Rashcliffe Mills supplies 70% of the most expensive fine quality worsteds to leading Italian fashion labels, as well as to the US and the Far East. Taylor & Lodge is also an important supplier to the Middle East, not just for ultra lightweight suiting but also for the superfine "dishdash" worn by Arab potentates over their traditional robes. "This is the most expensive piece we have ever made" is an oft-repeated remark at cloth fairs (usually referring to an ultra smooth lightweight cashmere or Vicuna suiting); the result of many man-hours spent on design and development to achieve a rare level of quality. Many of Taylor & Lodge's special orders are woven for specific customers in America and Japan.

ADDRESS
TAYLOR & LODGE, Rashcliffe Mills, Albert Street, Lockwood, Huddersfield, West Yorkshire HD1 3PE. Tel. +44 148 442 3231.

W.T. JOHNSON & SONS

Before the weaver goes to market one vital operation is necessary for both the appearance and substance of the cloth: finishing. W.T. Johnson & Sons, founded in 1910, is still a family company exploiting to the full the famous "Huddersfield factor." The Yorkshire mills are famed for the profoundly soft quality of the local water supply; "a fabric finisher's dream" as the company brochure proclaims. The present chief executive, Paul Johnson, says "we are immensely proud to be still building on the uncompromising tradition of quality my great grandfather began over ninety years ago." The company consistently explores new processes and technologies with local universities and chemical companies to produce unique finishes for a variety of textiles. The company currently promotes qualities such as Coolstretch, Silvershield, Nonobloc and V.V.Finish.

ADDRESS
W.T. JOHNSON & SONS, Bankfield Mills, Moldgreen, Huddersfield, West Yorkshire, HD5 9BB. www.wtjohnson.co.uk

DICTIONARY OF SAVILE ROW TAILORING TERMS AND SLANG

THE BASICS

Bespoke A suit made on or around Savile Row bespoken (custom made, in the US) to the customer's specifications. A bespoke suit (bespoken by the customer) is cut by an individual, for an individual and made by highly skilled individual craftsmen. The pattern is made specifically for the customer and the finished garment will take a minimum of fifty-two hours' work and at least three fittings.

Cutter The "front-of-house" craftsman who measures, cuts and fits the garment. The cutter is the architect rather than the builder. Cutters are usually employed by the house and work in the shop front.

Guv'nor The proprietor of a bespoke tailoring house on or around Savile Row.

Made-to-measure/personally tailored A made-to-measure suit is cut from a standard pattern and amended to suit the contours of the individual, but is ordinarily factory cut and made. Alternatively, a completed suit is altered to fit the customer more closely.

Master tailor In its strictest sense, a master tailor is the director or owner of a tailoring firm who is also a skilled tailor and/or cutter.

Striker A term for an undercutter or assistant to the cutter.

Tailor The hands that actually make the garment. Tailors are very rarely employed fulltime by the bespoke house. Although the largest Savile Row firms do have fulltime in-house tailors, the majority of tailors are out workers who are paid per completed garment.

TECHNICAL TERMS

Balance Adjustment of back and front lengths of a jacket to harmonize with the posture of a particular figure.

Baste Garment roughly assembled for the first fitting. Baste stitches are then ripped open and reset on the body of the customer.

Basting Tacking with long stitches to hold garment parts together.

Block Paper template of the basic pattern shape of the customer.

Bundle Individual pattern pieces of cloth before rolled into a "bundle" by the cutters in preparation for tailoring.

Canvas A cloth usually made from cotton, flax, hemp or jute and used for providing strength or firmness inside the jacket.

Coat Savile Row still insists on calling a jacket a "coat."

Draft Sketch or measured plan of a garment.

Fusing Use of chemicals and heat to weld the interlining to outer fabric. Bespoke tailors, who stitch the canvas into the coat, frown upon this practice and consider it a shortcut.

Gorge Where the collar is attached to the coat.

Interlining Material positioned between the lining and the outer fabric to provide bulk or warmth. The interlining can correct the silhouette of a man whose body is anything but of classical proportion.

Rock of eye A master tailor's instinct for cutting as opposed to the technical rules of a cutting system.

Scye The armhole or "arm's eye."

Skirt Part of the jacket that hangs below the waist.

Vent The opening at either side of the skirt or in the center back that allows for movement. Its origins lie in equestrian tailoring.

TOOLS

Baby Stuffed cloth pad on which the tailor works his cloth.

Banger Piece of wood with a handle used to draw out steam and smooth cloth during ironing.

Board Tailor's workbench.

Darky Sleeve board.

Dolly Roll of wet material used as a sponge to dampen cloth.

Goose iron Hand iron heated over a naked flame. The weight of the hand irons of old prevented women from gaining employment as pressers.

Mangle Sewing machine.

SLANG

Balloon A tailor's week without work or pay.

Basting up a snarl Starting an argument (not uncommon in tailor's workshops, rare on the cutting floor and a criminal offence in the shop front).

Bodger Crude work of an inexperienced or shoddy cutter or tailor.

Boot Loan until payday. Some tailors would get the boot by pawning bolts of cloth.

Bunce A trade perk.

Bushelmen A journeyman who alters or repairs.

Cabbage Left over material that was formerly sold to a scrap man by the ounce.

Cat's face A small shop opened by a cutter starting out on his own; rarely on ground floor premises and never on Savile Row.

Chuck a dummy To faint. Comparable to a mannequin falling over.

Clapham junction A draft with numerous alterations or additions. Clapham Junction is a London train station where many lines meet.

Codger A tailor who does up old suits.

Cork The guv'nor.

Crib Large scrap of cloth left over from a job large enough to make a pair of trousers.

Crushed beetle Badly made buttonhole.

Cutting turf Clumsy or unskilled work.

Dead . . . a dead horse A job that has been paid for in advance.

Doctor Alterations tailor.

Drag . . . in the drag Working behind time.

Drummer Trouser maker.

Hip stay The wife.

Jeff A cutter/tailor who makes the garment from pattern to finish.

Kicking Looking for another job.

Kicking your heels No work to do.

Kill A spoiled job that has to be thrown away.

Kipper A female tailor, so named because they sought work in pairs to avoid unwelcome admirers.

Mungo Cloth cuttings collected to be sold to a ragman.

On the cod Gone drinking. A time-honored and popular pastime on and around the Row.

Pig An unclaimed garment.

Pig sale A sale of uncollected garments by the bespoke house.

Pigged A lapel that curls after some wear.

Pinked . . . a pinked job Making with extreme care for an especially critical or important customer.

Pork A misfit rejected by a customer.

P.T. (rubbing in a P.T.) Doing private work in spare time such as lunch hours or weekends.

Schmutter A Jewish expression for a piece of poor cloth or a poor garment (a bit of schmutter).

Skiffle A job needed doing in a hurry.

Skipping it Making the stitches too big to save time and effort.

Small seams Warning call when someone being discussed enters the workroom.

Soft sew An easily worked cloth.

Tab Fussy, difficult customer.

Trotter Fetcher and carrier or messenger.

Tweed merchant Tailor who does easy work.

Thipping the cat Traveling around and working in private houses or offices.

Courtesy of Savile Row Bespoke and Richard Walker's *The Savile Row Story*.

BIBLIOGRAPHY

AMIES, HARDY. *The Englishman's Suit*. London: Quartet Books, 1994.

ANTONGIAVANNI, NICHOLAS. *The Suit: A Machiavellian Approach to Men's Style*. New York, Collins, 2006.

BONAMI, FRANCESCO, MARIA LUISA FRISA and STEFANO TONCHI, ed. *Uniform: Order and Disorder*. Milan–Florence: Charta–Fondazione Pitti Immagine Discovery, 2003.

BOYER, G. BRUCE. *Fred Astaire Style*. New York: Assouline, 2005.

BRESLER, FENTON. *Napoleon III: A Life*. London: Harper Collins, 2000.

BRET, DAVID. *Valentino: A Dream of Desire*. London: Robson Books, 1998.

BREWARD, CHRISTOPHER, EDWINA EHRMAN and CAROLINE EVANS. *The London Look: Fashion from Street to Catwalk*. New Haven & London, Yale University Press, 2005, in association with the Museum of London.

CAMPBELL, UNA. 300 Years of Cerimonial Dress. London: Ede & Ravenscroft Ltd., 1989.

CHIARINI, MARCO, ed. *Pitti Palace: All the Museums, All the Works*. Livorno: Firenze Musei/Sillabe, 2001.

CICOLINI, ALICE. *The New English Dandy*. New York: Assouline, 2005.

COHN, NIK. *Today There Are No Gentlemen: The Change in Englishmen's Clothes since the War*. London: Weidenfeld & Nicholson, 1971.

COOK, ANDREW. *Prince Eddy: The King Britain Never Had*. London: Tempus, 2006.

COPE, ALFRED, ed. *Cope's Royal Cavalcade of the Turf*. London: David Cope Ltd, 1953.

DECHARNE, MAX. *King's Road: The Rise and Fall of the Hippest Street in the World*. London: Phoenix, 2006.

DOBBS, BRIAN. *The Last Shall Be First: The Colourful Story of John Lobb, the St. James's Bootmaker*. London: Elm Tree Books/Hamish Hamilton, 1972.

DUKE OF WINDSOR. *A King's Story: The Memoirs of the Duke of Windsor*. 1951. Nuova edizione, London: Trafalgar Square Publishing, 1998.

FOULKES, NICHOLAS. *Turnbull & Asser*. London: Brompton Press, 1997.

FRISA, MARIA LUISA, and STEFANO TONCHI, ed. *Excess: Fashion and the Underground in the '80*. Milan–Florence: Charta–Fondazione Pitti Immagine Discovery, 2004.

GELARDI, JULIA. *Born to Rule: Granddaughters of Victoria, Queens of Europe*. London: Headline, 2004.

GORMAN, PAUL. *The Look: Adventures in Rock & Pop Fashion*. London: Adelita, 2006.

HOWARTH, STEPHEN. *Henry Poole, Founders of Savile Row: The Making of a Legend*. Honiton: Bene Factum Publishing, 2003.

KELLY, IAN. *Beau Brummell: The Ultimate Dandy*. London: Hodder, 2005.

KING, GREG. *The Duchess of Windsor: The Uncommon Life of Wallis Simpson*. London: Aurum, 2000.

LAVER, JAMES. *Costume and Fashion: A Concise History*. Concluding chapter by Christina Probert. London: Thames & Hudson, 1969.

McDOWELL, COLIN. *The Man of Fashion: Peacock Males & Perfect Gentlemen*. London: Thames & Hudson, 1997.

MRS. HUMPHREY ("Madge" of "Truth"). *Manners for Men*. London: James Bowden, 1897.

O'Connor, Patrick. *The Amazing Blonde Woman: Dietrich's Own Style*. London: Bloomsbury, 1991.

PAYNE, GRAHAM, and Sheridan Morley, ed. *The Noel Coward Diaries*. London: Phoenix Granta, 1982.

POPE-HENNESSY, JAMES. *Queen Mary 1867-1953*. London: Phoenix, 1959.
The Rogers Collection. Auction catalogue, Sotheby's, London, January 28–29–30, 1998.
London: Sotheby's, 1998.
TITMAN, GEORGE A., ed. *Dress & Insignia Worn at His Majesty's Court*. London: Harrison &
Sons Ltd, 1937.
TORREGROSSA, RICHARD. *Cary Grant: A Celebration of Style*. London: Aurum Press, 2006.
VAN DER KISTE, JOHN. *George V's Children*. Stroud: Sutton Publishing, 1991.
VICKERS, HUGO. *Cecil Beaton: The Authorized Biography*. London: Weidenfeld and Nicholson,
1985.
WALKER, RICHARD. *The Savile Row Story: An Illustrated History*. London: Prion, 1988.
WATT, JUDITH, ed. *The Penguin Book of Twentieth-Century Fashion Writing*. London:
Viking, 1999.

Extracts and images from *Tailor & Cutter, Cloth & Clothes, Men's Wear* and *Man About Town* courtesy of the EMap Archive, held by the London College of Fashion.

The following publications were consulted: *AnOtherMan, Arena Homme +, Esquire, Fashion Inc, GQ, GQ Style, L'Uomo Vogue, V Man, Vogue UK, Vogue Hommes, Men's Vogue* and *Wallpaper.*

Sincere thanks to Alistair O'Neill, Research Fellow at the London College of Fashion, for introducing the author to the EMap Archive, for his kind permission to lend an important personal collection of Tommy Nutter suits to exhibition and for agreeing to cast an expert eye over the text for *The London Cut*.